AND HE
WEPT

JAMES D. BREWER

And He Wept
Copyright © 2023 by James D. Brewer

ISBN: 979-8988147152 (sc)
ISBN: 979-8988147169 (e)

Riverview Press

info@riverview-press.com
www.riverview-press.com

The ultimate determinant in the struggle that is now going on in the world will not be bombs and rockets but a test of wills and ideas, a trial of spiritual resolve, the values we hold, the beliefs we cherish, the ideals to which we are dedicated. Ronald Reagan

I believe in Christianity as I believe that the sun has risen not only because I see it, but because by it I see everything else. C.S. Lewis

Our world stands at the threshold of eternity. I hope and pray that the message of this book will serve as a wake-up call to its readers.

Proverbs 14:12

God Bless,

Jim

Contents

Acknowledgements

This book is dedicated to Maggie, my dear wife and partner in life. Maggie inspired me and cheered me on, sometimes she pushed me on.

Thank you, Sweet Maggie.

This book may never have been completed without the urgings of Pat Lewis who gently pushed me on.

This book may never have been published without the diligence of a dear friend, Janet Olexy. Her excellent journalistic expertise and her willingness to read, edit, re-read and edit is immensely appreciated.

Thank you, Janet.

Preface

In 2017 my wife Maggie and I had recently returned from our 4th trip to Nairobi, Kenya, where we served for three months in 2017 as short-term missionaries with Africa Inland Mission (AIM). Our entire time in Kenya was spent serving and ministering to the people of Kibera. Kibera is the largest slum on the African continent and the second largest in the world. It is located on the southwest edge of Nairobi, about 3 miles from the center of the capital city. Kibera is a community in great need.

In reality, Kibera is a self-sustaining community of people, many of whom have jobs and work outside the community, although most jobs offer minimal pay that barely sustains them. Most of them live in survival mode, not unlike many in our country today. There are many homeless, unable to afford housing, so their choice of where to live is limited. These people are trapped in a life of poverty. Their only hope to break the bonds of poverty and illiteracy is through education. Parents are desperate to see that their children receive an education which will allow them to get jobs, thereby offering them the opportunity to move out of the slum and the possibility of living a productive life that is not burdened by the shame of poverty.

While working in the slum, I began to take notice of how the people we interacted with daily had a kind of admirable dignity. People of Kibera have little in the way of material possessions compared with people in the U.S.A., even less than those Americans who fall into our government's recognized category of poverty, yet there is an unmistakable joy in the hearts of the residents of Kibera, and they are grateful for what they have. Their clothing is worn, but it is clean; their tin-roofed mud homes are small, and scantily furnished, but neat as a pin and clean. The average Kiberan takes pride in what little they have; they take care of their home and possessions, and their children are very respectful of their elders.

Look around and take note of our society. I don't think it is a stretch of the imagination to say that a large percentage of Americans do not exhibit joy in their lives and, by and large, we are not grateful for what we have, i.e., our material possessions. We always seem to be ill-content with what we have; we always want bigger . . . better! All things considered; we do not take care of what we have. We are a "throw away" society. Many children are ill-behaved and disrespectful to one another and to their elders. In other words, our children are spoiled and so are a large percentage of adults/parents. Have we come so far that we have lost respect for ourselves?

Have we reached a point in our society where young people are willing to compromise their morals and ideals for success? Have the goals of our culture slipped so low that we have developed an "all or nothing" approach, doing whatever it takes to obtain our perceived success?

Unfortunately, life-long desires soon become old and need to be replaced by another want or desire. This scenario repeats itself again and again in the lives of many people today, both young and old. We search for something to fill the emptiness in our lives, and all too often we run into hopelessness. We are by nature selfish and self-centered. The book of James teaches us: "You lust and do not have; so you commit murder. You are envious and cannot obtain; so you fight and quarrel. You do not have because you do not ask." (4:2)

How then is it that many of the people of Kibera have joy in their hearts, even though, from the American point of view, they are helpless, and their lives are hopeless?

My experience in Africa has caused me to take greater notice of what I see as the downward spiral of our great country, our society, and its morals. Many people today have surrendered the capability to think for themselves. We are in a dark place. Our politicians want to focus on the economy. The problem lies much deeper. Wake up America . . . it may not be too late!!

"If My people who are called by My name will humble themselves, and pray and seek My face, and turn from their wicked ways, then I will hear from heaven, and will forgive their sin and heal their land." (2 Chronicles 7:14)

CHAPTER 1

Newton's Laws of Motion

Sir Isaac Newton defined three physical laws that form the basis for classical mechanics. They describe the relationship between the forces acting on a body and its motion due to those forces. They have been expressed in several different ways over nearly three centuries, and can be summarized as follows:

First law: Every object moves in a straight line and at an unchanged velocity, unless acted upon by a force.

Second law: The acceleration of an object is dependent upon two variables - the net force acting upon the object and the mass of the object.

Third law: For every action, there is an equal and opposite reaction.

Believe it or not, Newton's law can be applied to what we are seeing unfold in the values that our culture holds today as opposed to the values on which this great country was founded.

Every action taken in this life has an equal and opposite reaction that shall come as a direct consequence of whatever was done to disturb the actual balance; this is as true in nature as it is in life.

The maxim does not mention how long it might take to correct the imbalance caused by repeated bad choices, but the fact that consequences will follow bad choices cannot be disputed. The good people of this world far outnumber the criminal elite and the would-be controllers of our lives; people should remember this and begin to act accordingly. Don't just go with the flow or be hyped by the latest and greatest. Dare to be different and think for yourself. The conservatives of this world far outnumber the liberal thinkers. A poignant question is, why do we allow the much smaller number of liberals and radicals to have such a negative influence on our society at large?

This is what I have learned in my life: YOU are responsible for your life. No one but you is responsible for your life. You cannot blame your parents; you cannot blame your school classmates; you cannot blame the unfairness that sometimes comes in life.

You are responsible for the energy you create for yourself (Newton's First Law).

You are responsible for the energy you bring to others (Newton's Second Law).

You are responsible for knowing the truth, which is an absolute (Newton's Third Law).

In today's society, truth has evolved from an absolute truth to a "relative" truth. In other words, what is true for you is not necessarily true for me.

Newton's third law states that mutual forces of action

(absolute truth) and reaction (relative truth) are equally opposite and co-linear, meaning that neither will agree with the other point of view, but will continue to move forward in opposing directions. To whatever end, I do not know. I do know, however, that in the end of it all, absolute truth will win over the relative point of view. How do I know? I know because God is real, and His Word is unchanging and infallible; it is the only absolute humankind has and can always rely on. His Word tells us how all will end. I, for one, want the energy that I create for myself and bring to others to be in line with the truth that God has established in His Word.

WHERE DO YOU STAND?

This book is meant to draw attention to what I see as the continued unraveling of our society and the values that we once held dear.

I am a Veteran of the Vietnam War and I know first-hand that Vietnam War was one of the most unpopular wars in which Americans ever fought. There is no reckoning the cost. The toll in suffering, sorrow, in rancorous national turmoil can never be tabulated. No one wants to ever see America so divided again.

I believe the disintegration of these values accelerated during the era of the Vietnam War and have accelerated even more in the last half of this decade namely, from 2017 to 2022.

I believe the United States of America was established by the divine providence of God, our Creator.

Religious persecution sent the first successful colonizers on a journey which led them to America during the fall of 1620. On November 9th of that year, the Pilgrims first sighted land. They had originally intended to disembark on the coast of Virginia, where they had a land grant from England. However, because of violent storms, which proved to be providential, they were driven off course and forced to land in what is known today as Cape Cod Bay, Massachusetts.

These events draw me to the conclusion that the tyranny our forefathers faced, and the misfortune of landing much farther north than they had planned, were not just by coincidence; they were predestined by the Architect of our universe. These men and women set out for North America to start a new life and a new society that would be guided by self-determined regulations that would establish reasonable and just laws, thereby reconciling liberty with law: i.e., freedom to choose, but guided by a Christian-based decree.

The principles that shaped our culture were noble and praiseworthy. But in the last century, especially in the 1960's, we experienced inconceivable changes that have brought endless challenges to the ideals that once made our nation great. The moralities this country was founded on have been forsaken. The result of these upheavals has been the breakdown of law, annihilation of the Spirit, and the unleashing of evil, the likes of which brought about the total destruction of Sodom and Gomorrah.

The response of conservative Christianity has been, in effect, a scream in the dark. A morally bankrupt society has chosen to simply discount the conservative call for the return of ethical behavior in our Congressional representatives. Our mainstream media equates Evangelical Christianity with fanatical religious kooks. In the worlds of business and education, pronouns referring to a person's gender are no longer allowed to be used. When I donate blood these days one of the questions is not "What is your gender?" Instead that question has been replaced by, "What gender do you identify with?"

Many people have chosen to idolize celebrities whose drug abuse and sexual promiscuity are continuously lauded in the media as some sort of a badge of honor. These celebrity antics are the focus of news reports on an almost daily basis. The poor choices these celebrities make are not reported as such. Instead, the picture is painted of a poor distraught person of privilege who has been broken by the pressures of life. They tend to blame others around them or circumstances, or people in their past.

Basically, this book is broken down into three sections: Present, Past, and Future.

PAST

We must examine the influences that have shaped our culture to what it is we see today.

PRESENT

The founding fathers developed unique, intricate, and well-thought-out documents, and put them in place to guide the people and leaders of this country. They created the Constitution and the Bill of Rights as an act of foresight; to protect America from self-destruction.

FUTURE

Finally, we must consider where we might possibly end up as a nation, as a page in the history books, or should I say, as only a footnote on a page in the history books.

Despite the aura of omnipotence most empires, if we project a closer look at their history, reminds us that *they were and we are fallible and fragile organisms.* I found an interesting quote from Alexander Fraser Tytler, Lord Woodhouselee (October 15, 1747 - January 5, 1813). He was a Scottish-born British lawyer, writer, and history professor at the University of Edinburgh.

In the year of 1770 Tyler is quoted, having said this about democracy:

"A democracy is always temporary in nature; it simply cannot exist as a permanent form of government. A democracy will continue to exist up until the time that voters discover that they can vote themselves generous gifts from the public treasury. From that moment on, the majority always votes for the candidates who promise the most benefits from the public treasury, with the result that every democracy will finally collapse over loose fiscal policy, which is always followed by a dictatorship. The average age of the world's greatest civilizations from the beginning of history has been about 200 years. During those 200 years, these nations always progressed through the following sequence: from bondage to spiritual faith; from spiritual faith to great courage; from courage to liberty; from liberty to abundance; from abundance to complacency; from complacency to apathy; from apathy to dependence; from dependence back into bondage."

So delicate is the ecology of power that, when things start to go truly bad, empires regularly unravel with unholy speed.

The obituary for our great country could possibly read - United States of America: Born – 1776; Died – *Your best guess?*

Does this sound familiar? It is a perfect parallel to where our country has regressed. What is taking place in our country today has been allowed, has been caused by society not considering God's intended plan for this great nation. We all need to consider God's Word, not follow public opinions that can lead us down the treacherous path to destruction. The founding fathers carefully and prayerfully constructed the Constitution, guided by God's own words.

But, have no doubt - when Washington's global dominion finally ends, there will be turmoil for Americans in every walk of life. As European nations have discovered, imperial decline tends to have a remarkably demoralizing impact on a society. As the economy cools, political temperatures rise, often sparking serious domestic unrest.

Available economic, educational, and military data indicate that, when it comes to U.S. global power, negative trends will build up rapidly, possibly by 2023, and are likely to reach a critical mass no later than 2030. The American Century, proclaimed so triumphantly at the start of World War II, will be tattered and fading by 2025, its eighth decade, and could be history by 2030.

Is it too late? I think not! We must get back to where we once were. I know that God can work all things for good; He promises us that in the Bible: "And we know that in all things God works for the good of those who love him, who have been called according to his purpose." (Romans 8:28)

As long as the people of this nation remain stiff-necked and continue to turn away from God and the truth of God's Word, He will not rescue us from ourselves.

I hope it is not too late for us to ask God to grant mercy on our nation, a nation who has turned its back on Him. We must pray *incessantly* for mercy and turn our faces back to God: turn the face of our nation back to God.

We must read and remember - 2 Chronicles: 7:14: "If My people who are called by My name will humble themselves, and pray and seek My face, and turn from their wicked ways, then I will hear from heaven, and will forgive their sin and heal their land."

CHAPTER 2

The Divine Providence of God

Our nation's independence was allowed and established by the grace of God to come about because of the godly men who founded it. God intended our nation to be a lighthouse to the world. From the very start and we have been more blessed by God than any nation in the history of the world, with the sole exception possibly of Israel which was and is His chosen nation.

Our nation has been the leader of the free world for a long time and has produced many brilliant inventors, scientists, preachers, and other great people who have been the envy of the world. Initially our nation obeyed God and thanked God for His blessings on this country by sending missionaries into the world to spread the gospel and reach people for Jesus. Missions' organizations have sent countless numbers of missionaries to foreign shores. Our nation has fallen away from Jesus. In recent decades we have seen missionaries sent to us from countries such as South Korea and Brazil. The United States is ripe for harvest, as it is filled with many unsaved people. Many today no longer identify as Christians; how sad, considering this is what our nation was founded on.

The Mayflower Compact is a document that was written and signed November 1620 on the British ship, the Mayflower, prior to its landing at Plymouth, Massachusetts. It was the first framework of government written and enacted in the territory that is now the United States of America and it remained in force until 1691 when Plymouth Colony became part of Massachusetts Bay Colony.

The purpose of the Mayflower Compact was to establish basic law and order in the colony. The document was intended to be not just a contract between the colonists but also between themselves and God.

The following is the full text of the Mayflower Compact:

"In the name of God, Amen."

We whose names are underwritten, the loyal subjects of our dread Sovereign Lord King James, by the Grace of God, of Great Britain, France, and Ireland King, Defender of the Faith, etc.

Having undertaken, for the glory of God, and advancement of the Christian faith, and honor of our king and country, a voyage to plant the first colony in the northern parts of Virginia, do by these presents solemnly and mutually in the presence of God and one of another, covenant, and combine ourselves together into a civil body politic, for our better ordering and preservation, and furtherance of the ends aforesaid; and by virtue hereof to enact, constitute, and frame such just and equal Laws, Ordinances, Acts, Constitutions, and

*Offices from time to time, as shall be thought most meet
and convenient for the general good of the Colony; unto
which we promise all due submission and obedience.
In witness whereof we have hereunder subscribed our
names at Cape Cod, the 11th of November, in the year of
the reign of our Sovereign Lord King James, of England,
France and Ireland eighteenth and of Scotland fifty-
fourth. Anno Domini 1620.*

*John Carver, Edward Tilley, Degory Priest, William
Bradford, John Tilley, Thomas Williams, Edward
Winslow, Francis Cooke, Gilbert Winslow, William
Brewster, Thomas Rogers, Edmund Margesson, Isaac
Allerton, Thomas Tinker, Peter Brown, Myles Standish,
John Rigsdale, Richard Britteridge, John Alden, Edward
Fuller, George Soule.*

The Mayflower Compact was superseded when the
Pilgrims obtained a patent from the Council of New
England for their settlement at Plymouth in 1621. At that
time, they became part of the Massachusetts Bay Colony,
which became a royal colony with a mixed government,
the colony known as the Province of Massachusetts
Bay. A mixed government meant it was partly a charter
government and partly a royal government, with the
Governor appointed by the Crown. This mixed government
came to an end less than 100 years later when the colony
won its legislative and economic freedom from Britain
during the American Revolution.

THE TRANSITION

The Mayflower Compact was an early, successful
attempt at democracy and undoubtedly played a role
in future colonists seeking permanent independence

from British rule and shaping the nation that eventually became the United States of America

God gives freedom to people. Many brave men and women have died for our nation in our wars, but true freedom only comes from God and His son Jesus, especially for those who are saved and have received Jesus as their Savior. Only those who are saved will have true freedom from spiritual death and independence from Satan. Jesus will save all of those who call upon him by admitting they are sinners in need of a Savior. All of us have sinned and sin leads to death (Romans 3:23) "For all have sinned and fall short of the glory of God." (Romans 6:23) "For the wages of sin is death, but the gracious gift of God is eternal life in Christ Jesus our Lord."

(Romans 6:6-9) "Knowing this, that our old self was crucified with Him, in order that our body of sin might be done away with, so that we would no longer be slaves to sin; for the one who has died is freed from sin." Now if we have died with Christ, we believe that we shall also live with Him, knowing that Christ, having been raised from the dead, is never to die again; death no longer is master over Him."

The Constitution of the United States is the supreme law of the United States of America. The first three Articles of the Constitution establish the rules and separate the powers of the three branches of the federal government: a legislature, Congress; an executive branch led by the President; and the federal judiciary headed by the Supreme Court.

Our forefathers, the architects of our government and our Constitution, were God fearing people. They poured themselves into creating a system of governance to prevent what we see happening before our very eyes, namely that the wolves have slipped into the pews of our nation's churches, and they have been allowed to do so by the wolves who have taken over our government.

The Constitution was written in 1787. It was penned, edited, redrafted, and finally ratified on September 17th, 1787.

Some believe our Constitution has seen its better days. Most certainly, it is our nation's founding document. To many it is a sacred text, the oldest written national constitution still in effect anywhere in the world, but its influence is diminished by the images we and the rest of the world see on our television screens. Recently, nightly news reports on all channels were dominated by images of the "occupy movement" with protesters showing themselves to be unruly anarchists, some defecating in public places, some of them burning flags and copies of our Constitution.

Could it be that even casual observers of some Americans' actions are able to perceive that our Constitution means little or nothing to them? Why should they adopt our governing roadmap when many don't even bother to respect it, to abide by it?

Of late there have been rumblings of redrafting the Constitution. I, for one, am hugely against any such attempt. We have weakened the Constitution through many of the amendments to it. We have so screwed-up our ways of thinking, what makes us think the modernizing of our "sacred document" would be the answer?

Our dilemma is that on one hand we have people who believe that if we decided to rewrite our constitution, the right wing would likely destroy what few freedoms we have. On the other hand, there are people who believe in our Constitution that say beware of the elitist left forging chains of slavery by making us, in every move they make, beholden and dependent on the state.

CHAPTER 3

How Good Were The "Good Old Days?"

THE 1920S - CHANGING ATTITUDES AND VALUES

The prosperity of the 1920s brought a change in lifestyle for many Americans: more people owned their own homes and cars. There was more time for hobbies and leisure time activities, and people had more money to spend on their pleasures. The entertainment industry grew; there were dance halls and new clubs opening almost weekly. There were changes in social attitudes as well. People were influenced by what they heard on the radio and saw at the movie theaters. The equality movement and the rebellion of the youth in the 1920s exemplified the complete disregard of authority and responsible behavior practiced by past generations.

On January 17, 1920, the Volstead Act was passed. The law commonly known as prohibition, banned the manufacture, transportation, and sale of alcoholic beverages. The law was repealed on December 5, 1931.

Prohibition encouraged wild partying where alcohol flowed freely and the fact that it was illegal made it all the more exciting. It *was*, after all, the 'Roaring Twenties'. The law ushered in organized crime. Along with creating an army of federal agents, the Volstead Act stipulated that individual states should enforce Prohibition within their own borders. Governors resented the added strain on their public coffers, however, and many neglected to appropriate any money toward policing the alcohol ban. Maryland never even enacted an enforcement code, and eventually earned a reputation as one of the most stubbornly anti-Prohibition states in the Union.

America's first radio station, Station KDKA, was started in 1920. The radio quickly became an important part of life. In just 10 years 40% of all homes in the USA had a radio set. The radio gave Americans access to new types of music from dance to jazz. It created a national habit of listening to sporting events that they could not go to see. Sports personalities, such as baseball stars, became national figures because of the radio.

Clubs and dancehalls became enormously popular in the 1920s. The slow, formal with little close contact dances of pre-war America were replaced by fast dances like the Charleston and more rhythmic dances that had an openly sexual element to them. Dancing had such a dramatic effect that many people condemned it.

The 1920s has been called the 'Jazz Age'. Jazz and blues music dominated all other music at this time, and it had a tremendous impact on the young. It fed into dancehalls, popular music, and stage musicals. Older people saw it as a corrupting influence linked to sexual excess.

One of the biggest areas of change and controversy was sexual morals. Sex outside marriage became more common, and contraceptive advice was openly available for the first time. A big gap was developing between the attitudes of young people and their parents.

Young Americans visited the movie theater two and sometimes three times per week. They were greatly affected by what they saw on the screen and by the lives of the 'stars' off screen. People wanted to know what their favorite stars were wearing and doing, and they wanted to copy the fads and fashions in their own lives. Studio publicity agents made sure that the magazines got all the information they needed to keep their readers interested.

As viewpoints became more worldly and lifestyles more adventure some, clothing became more daring. Women's hemlines rose from ankle length to knee length.

As all aspects of life were changing, Americans were becoming less connected to organized religion. Instead of attending church services, many Americans spent weekends riding in automobiles and watching movies. Hobbies became more frivolous as the nation became preoccupied with fads ranging from crossword puzzles to dance marathons. A youth culture arose, and teenagers indulged in pastimes such as petting parties, shocking their more conservative elders.

The much freer sex of the 1920s horrified many older Americans. They blamed movies for their blatant use of sex symbols such as Clara Bow and Rudolf Valentino.

THE 1930S - THE GREAT DEPRESSION

The Great Depression was a worldwide economic collapse that began in 1929 and lasted roughly a decade.

It was a disaster that touched the lives of millions of Americans, from investors who saw their fortunes vanish overnight, to factory workers and clerks who found themselves unemployed and desperate for a way to feed their families. Nearly 4 million people were unemployed and there were no jobs to be found.

Between 1929 and 1932 the annual income of the average American family was reduced by 40%, from $2,300 to just $1,500. Money was scarce because of the depression, so people did what they could to make their lives happy. It was difficult to keep food on the table.

On March 31, 1933, President Franklin D. Roosevelt signed legislation to create the Civilian Conservation Corps, the first of the New Deal agencies. The CCC employed young men and gave them an opportunity to develop new skills and prepare them for future employment as the nation recovered from the Great Depression. Although there are no official records, estimates of the number of young men who participated in the nine-year program reached approximately three million. Congress extended the program to include African Americans, Native Americans, and World War I veterans. Enrollees performed a variety of conservation activities including reforestation, soil conservation, road construction, flood and fire control, and agricultural management. The CCC also completed a number of tasks associated with the development and construction of state and national parks.

Most of the Americans who were won over to the consumption ethic of the 1920s had been brought up on the traditional values, struggled to hold fast to those values which were quickly being abandoned. Large numbers of Americans turned against greed and excessive individualism and returned more to such ideals as prudence, and community cooperation ideals.

In the Great Depression the American dream had become a nightmare. What was once the land of opportunity was now the land of desperation. What was once the land of hope and optimism had become the land of despair. The American people were questioning all the principles on which they had based their lives - democracy, capitalism, and individualism. The best hope for a better life was California. Many Dust Bowl farmers packed their families into cars, tied their few possessions on the back, and sought work in the agricultural fields or cities of the West - their role as independent landowners gone forever. Instead of advancement, survival became the keyword. Institutions, attitudes, and lifestyles changed in this decade, but democracy prevailed. Democracies such as Germany and Italy fell to dictatorships, but the United States and its Constitution survived.

The 1930's were a perilous time for public education. With cash money in short supply parents were unable to provide their children with the necessary clothes, supplies, and textbooks (which were not furnished in some states) to attend school. Taxes, especially in rural areas, went unpaid. With the loss of revenue, school boards were forced to try numerous strategies to keep their districts operating. School terms were shortened. Teachers' salaries were cut. A new teacher was paid $40 a month for a five-month school year - and was very glad for the job! When a rural county in Arkansas was forced to charge tuition for one year in order to keep the schools open, some children were forced to drop out for that year. Some farmers were able to barter wood to fuel the classrooms' potbellied stoves for their children's tuition, thus enabling them to continue their education.

The famous Dick and Jane books that taught millions of children to read were first published in 1931. These primers introduced the students to reading with only one new word per page and a limited vocabulary per book. All who learned to read with these books still recall the "Look. See Dick. See Dick run."

Religious institutions across the United States had expanded their charitable efforts and their social reform campaigns, but the depression wiped out the support for that work just as Americans needed it most.

Despite the hardship of the Depression, Americans did not turn to religion for comfort. In fact, church attendance declined in the 1930s. This was partly because people were embarrassed when they were unemployed and partly because people moved around more and lost the "habit" of going to church. Understandably, contributions to churches also fell, leaving many churches in debt.

Many churches folded due to lack of financial support. The devastating effects of the Depression on local communities meant that individuals, families, and communities wrestled with deep theological questions together. Local communities reorganized around activism and engagement in pooling resources to help families and individuals in need. In other words, the bond between the church and community suffered as people turned to self-sustainment rather than crying out to God in prayer.

Movies were hot and parlor games and board games were popular. People gathered around radios to listen to the Yankees. Young people danced to the big bands. Franklin Roosevelt influenced Americans with his Fireside Chats. The golden age of the mystery novel continued as people escaped into books, reading writers like Agatha Christie,

Dashiell Hammett, and Raymond Chandler.

The stability of families was tested by the Great Depression. A progressive era in Hollywood filmmaking in the early 1930's and a lax code of censorship allowed sin to rule the movies. When sin ruled the movies, very little was off limits if film studios had their way in the four-year period from 1930 until 1934, now called the pre-code era, when film studios ramped up violence, sex, and sin to draw in audiences in this post silent movie era.

The downward spiral in morality continued, and the air crackled with sexual tension, petting parties were the norm among some groups of teens and young adults. Couples drank, mingled, and eventually started kissing, moving from partner to partner. What had started as a wild bohemian party was now something more intimate.

THE 1940S – A WORLD AT WAR

The 1940s were dominated by World War II. Although the US had been providing support to the Allies before this, it maintained neutrality until the attack on Pearl Harbor.

The United States officially entered World War II as a response to the bombing of Pearl Harbor in Hawaii by the Japanese on Dec. 7, 1941. The country had been keeping itself isolated from the global war; however, after the attack, the country declared war on Japan on Dec. 8, 1941. Germany and Italy, who had a pact with Japan declared war on the United States three days later on December 11. This meant the U.S. forces had to fight on two fronts: one in the Pacific and one in Europe.

Following the attacks, the U.S. military needed to mobilize quickly. Although President Franklin D. Roosevelt and Congress had implemented a draft in 1940, the draft was extended to all men ages 18 to 64 by 1942. During the war over 36 million men registered, giving the local draft boards an extremely large pool from which to work.

When the Depression ended and World War II began, families had to cope with new issues: housing shortages, lack of schools, and prolonged separation of families. World War II has been the bloodiest war in human history. Nobody has exact figures, but it is estimated that the U.S. lost 407,000 military deaths and around 12,000 civilian deaths (due to crimes of war and military activity such as bombings.) The total death count for all Americans amounted up to 420,000.

War production pulled our country out of the Great Depression; unemployment virtually disappeared. The effects of the war on the family unit were devastating.

Women were needed to replace men who had gone off to war, and so the first great exodus of women from the home to the workplace began. Women proved that they could do "men's" work and do it well. With men away to serve in the military and demands for war material increasing, manufacturing jobs opened up to women and upped their earning power. Yet women's employment was only encouraged as long as the war was on. Once the war was over, federal and civilian policies replaced women workers with men.

The wartime sacrifice of women in support of the war effort is often overlooked. As World War II raged on throughout Europe and the Pacific women stood in the gap, working in factories filling positions such as welders and machinists. Women worked in foundries to turn scrap metal into cannon barrels, rifle assemblies, wheels, and tracks for armored vehicles. Women were essential for the production of supplies and goods to support our fighting troops. My own mother worked in a factory as a machinist to help support the war effort by taking the place of a man who was called to serve our country by going to war.

Rationing affected the food Americans ate, the clothes they wore, the toys with which children played. Many items we take for granted today were rationed, meaning you could only buy the amount that was allowed by the government. In some cases, rationing was the only way to ensure that all citizens would have access to things needed for survival.

It is almost impossible to explain how much of an impact the war had on all aspects of life. Americans were not allowed to simply walk into a store and buy as much sugar, butter, or meat as they liked. They could no longer fill their gas tank whenever they wanted.

After the war, the men returned, having seen the rest of the world. No longer was the family farm an ideal; no longer would blacks accept lesser status. The GI Bill allowed more men than ever before to get a college education, except for African Americans. Women had to give up their jobs to the returning men, but they had tasted independence, and this did not set well.

The surrender of German forces occurred May 1945. Grand Admiral Karl Dönitz, who started peace negotiations May 5th and on May 7, 1945, authorized General Alfred Jodl to sign an unconditional surrender. The surrender of the Empire of Japan was announced on August 15, 1945, bringing the war to an end.

During the war years women ran households and raised

children alone, and some went to work in war industries. The results of the war-stricken state of society were that thousands of young people became "latchkey children" and rates of juvenile delinquency, unwed pregnancy, and truancy all rose. The family unit had suffered yet another setback.

THE 1950S – THE POST WAR BOOMS

The end of World War II brought thousands of young servicemen back to America to pick up their lives and start new families in new homes with new jobs. With an energy never before experienced, American industry expanded to meet peacetime needs. Americans began buying goods not available during the war, which created corporate expansion and jobs. Growth was everywhere. The baby boom was underway.

Though women, as a whole, had access to more jobs than ever before, they were paid far less than men, and most found themselves pressured to relinquish jobs to the male soldiers returning home at war's end. But something had permanently shifted: World War II empowered women to seek new opportunities and fight for equal pay in the decades to come.

Life in the "1950s America" was marked by economic growth, consumption, family, and conformity. Many Americans left the cities for the suburbs, where they enjoyed rising incomes, easy credit, and new products. Family became a powerful and efficient unit, with many women opting for lives as homemakers and men taking back the majority of the jobs. There was also a marriage boom, birth rate boom, and housing boom. However, not everything was peaceful and simple. The 1950s also saw the emergence of the teenager, rock and roll, and the civil rights movement, which challenged the culture of conformity and the existing state of affairs.

During the fifties, American education underwent dramatic and, for some, world shattering changes. Until 1954, an official policy of "Separate but Equal" educational opportunities for blacks had been determined to be the correct method to ensure that all children in America received an adequate and equal education in the public schools of the nation. In 1954, Chief Justice Earl Warren and other members of the Supreme Court wrote in Brown v. the Board of Education of Topeka Kansas that separate facilities for blacks did not make those facilities equal according to the Constitution. Integration was begun across the nation. In 1956, Autherine J. Lucy successfully enrolled in the University of Alabama at Tuscaloosa. In 1957, Elizabeth Eckford was the first black teenager to enter then all-white Arkansas school, Little Rock Central High School. Although integration took place quietly in most towns, the conflict at Central High School in Little Rock was the first of many confrontations in Arkansas which showed that public opinion on this issue was divided.

THE 1960S - CULTURAL DECADE

The sixties were the age of youth, as 70 million children from the post-war baby boom became teenagers and young adults. The movement away from the conservative fifties continued and eventually resulted in revolutionary ways of thinking and real change in the cultural fabric of American life. No longer content to follow in the footsteps of the generation ahead of them, young people wanted change. The changes affected education, values, lifestyles, laws, and entertainment. Many of the revolutionary ideas which began in the sixties are continuing to evolve today.

During the sixties, an estimated 850,000 "war babies" freshmen entered college; emergency living quarters were set up in dorm lounges, hotels, and trailer camps, college campuses became centers of debate and scenes of protest more than ever before. Great numbers of young males reached the military draft age of 18 yet were not eligible to voting age until 1971. This caused a struggle which played out on many campuses as the country became more involved in the Vietnam War. Young men were old enough to fight a war but not old enough to vote. The generation gap became a growing phenomenon that led to outbreaks of violent protests on college campuses and bombings of educational and business institutions. American flags were set on fire; Women's Lib held public bra burnings, and draft dodgers headed for Canada.

Increased immigration followed passage of the Immigration Act of 1965, which reformed an earlier policy that favored western Europeans. People from Third World countries came to this country in search of economic betterment or to escape political repression.

In 1966, James S. Coleman published the government sponsored Equality of Educational Opportunity, a landmark study that led the way to forced integration and busing in the 1970s.

Problems in secondary schools, discovered in the fifties, were being addressed in books such as James B. Conant's *The American High School Today*. A return to the teaching of basic thinking skills was seen to be part of the solution. In grade schools across the nation, phonics made a comeback as reading specialists tried to fix what went wrong in American education in the fifties.

And then there was Wood Stock. Who, living during that time, did not hear of the event? Woodstock Music and Art Fair was held during August 15–18, 1969, on Max Yasgur's dairy farm in Bethel, New York, United States, 40 miles southwest of the town of Woodstock. Billed as "an Aquarian Exposition: 3-days of Peace & Music" and alternatively referred to as the Woodstock Rock Festival, it attracted an audience of more than 400,000 attendees. Thirty-two acts performed outdoors despite sporadic rain. It was one of the largest music festivals in history.

The Woodstock audience was diverse and a reflection of the rapidly changing times. Some were hippies who felt alienated by a society immersed in materialism. In 1969, the country was deep into the controversial Vietnam War, a conflict that many young people vehemently opposed. It was also the era of the civil rights movement, a period of great protest and unrest. Woodstock was an opportunity for people to escape into music and spread a message of unity and peace.

Although the crowd at Woodstock experienced bad weather, muddy conditions and a lack of food, water and adequate sanitation, the overall vibe there was harmonious. Looking back, some people attribute the lack of violence to the large number of psychedelic drugs being used.

Others believe hippies were simply living out their mantra of "making love, not war." In fact, more than a few couples at Woodstock took that command literally and made love whenever and wherever the mood hit.

The widely used hallucinogenic drugs and the "free love" vibe also accompanied the youth movement. When one thinks of LSD, a very specific aesthetic probably leaps to mind: the psychedelic pink-and-orange swirls of the 60s; naked people with flowers in their hair; the shimmer of a sitar. Although its psychedelic properties were accidentally discovered in the lab by Albert Hofmann in 1943; LSD is still most strongly associated with hippies who embraced its mind-expanding properties.

In fact, the drug's after-effects have seeped through much of Western culture, from art to literature to, most obviously, music, which was never the same after Bob Dylan, The Beatles and Jimi Hendrix dropped acid. Whole genres have since flagged their debt to mind-altering substances: psychedelic rock, psytrance, acid house the latter hailing from that other spike in psych: 80s and 90s rave culture.

Freedom and change were the anthems of the 60s. It's not that family lost its importance, but over this decade families became less structured, family ties loosened, parents became more permissive, children became more independent and self-reliant, and family life became more complex. More latch-key children were raising themselves. The chasm between God and family continued to grow.

THE 1970S - VIETNAM WAR – NOVEMBER 1, 1955 – APRIL 30, 1975

The chaotic events of the '60s, including war and social change, seemed destined to continue into the '70s. Major trends included a growing disillusionment with government. First a Vice President and then a President resigned under threat of impeachment. The decade was marked by advances in civil rights, increased influence of the women's movement, a heightened concern for the environment, and increased space exploration. Many of the "radical" ideas of the '60s gained wider acceptance in the new decade and were mainstreamed into American life and culture. Amid war, social realignment and presidential impeachment proceedings, American culture flourished. Indeed, the events of the times were reflected in and became the inspiration for much of the music, literature, entertainment, and even fashion of the decade.

The Vietnam War was a long, drawn-out, and an atrocious war for everyone involved, particularly the Vietnamese civilians who were on the receiving end of much of the violence. Life was a mixed bag for the U.S. soldiers fighting in the Vietnam War.

The objectives of the war were unclear. One significant problem faced by Vietnam War soldiers was being engaged in a conflict without clear military objectives. There was no war front to advance, no safe region to defend, not even a well-defined theatre in which to operate.

The Vietnam conflict was a 360-degree war where any soldier – particularly Americans and Westerners – might encounter attacks, ambushes and booby traps at any place or time. It was a conflict where territory changed hands frequently, people moved freely, and their political loyalties were often unclear. Unlike earlier conflicts, such as both world wars, the Vietnam War was a shiftless and often vague struggle between a powerful conventional military force and a guerrilla army that operated in the shadows.

Two trends not directly related to education nonetheless heavily impacted the nation's schools and campuses during the Seventies. Social movements, particularly the anti-war movement, were highly visible on college and university campuses. The Kent State massacre occurred on May 4, 1970, when members of the Ohio National Guard opened fire on unarmed Kent State University students during a peace rally opposing the expanding involvement of the Vietnam War into Cambodia by United States military forces as well as protesting the National Guard presence on was the most devastating event, with four students gunned down by Ohio National Guardsmen attempting to stem the anti-war demonstrations.

During the 1970's the United States underwent some profound changes. The Vietnam War continued to divide the country even after the Paris Peace Accords. January 1973 put an end to U.S. military participation in the war. Roe v. Wade legalized abortion. Crime increased despite President Nixon's pledge to make law and order a top priority of his presidency.

Women, minorities, and gays increasingly demanded full legal equality and privileges in society. Women expanded their involvement in politics. The proportion of women in state legislatures tripled. Women surpassed men in college enrollment in 1979. However, the rising divorce rate left an increasing number of women as sole breadwinners and forced more and more of them into poverty. African Americans also made their presence felt as the number of black members in Congress increased, and cities such as Los Angeles, Detroit, and Atlanta elected their first African American mayors. Affirmative action became a controversial policy as minorities and women asserted their rights to jobs and quality education. Native Americans began to demand attention to their plight. In 1975 the Indian Self-Determination Act encouraged Indians to take control of their own education and promote their tribal customs.

After the 1973 resignation of Vice President Spiro T. Agnew, and the 1974 resignation of President Richard M.

Nixon, Gerald Ford, who at the time, held the position of House Speaker assumed the office of President of the United States (1974-1977), followed by and Jimmy Carter, President from (1977-1981).

The 1970s were a time of significant change in family structure in the United States. One of the most significant changes was the increase in one-person households and decreases in family size. While plenty of married people still had kids, the number of children per household declined dramatically.

The new independence of women and the new personal freedoms of youth enabled men and women to form healthier relationships and build more successful lives as singles.

Although the 1960s led to a questioning of religious institutions, causing a decline in regular attendance, the resulting decline in religion stopped by the end of the 1970s, when church attendance remained steady.

THE 1980S - THE ME GENERATION

The 1980s became the Me Generation of status seekers. During the 1980s, hostile takeovers, leveraged buyouts, and mega-mergers spawned a new breed of billionaire Icons. Donald Trump, Leona Helmsley, and Ivan Boesky exemplified the meteoric rise and fall of the rich and famous. "If you've got it, flaunt it" and "You can have it all!" were popular catch phrases. Forbes' list of 400 richest people became more important than its 500 largest companies. Binge buying and credit became a way of life and "Shop-Til you Drop" was the watchword. Labels were everything, even for teens. Tom Wolfe dubbed baby-boomers "the 'splurge generation." Video games, aerobics, minivans, camcorders, and talk shows became part of our lives. The decade began with double-digit inflation of 13.3%; unemployment rose to a shocking 10%. President Reagan declared a war on drugs; hospital costs rose, and we lost many of our finest talents to AIDS, which before the decade ended spread to black and Hispanic women. On the bright side, the US Constitution celebrated its 200th birthday. "Gone with the Wind" turned 50; ET phoned home; and in 1989 Americans gave $115,000,000,000 to charity. Internationally, at the very end of the decade the Berlin Wall was removed – leading to great changes for the decade to come! At the turn of the decade, many were happy to leave the spendthrift '80s for the '90s, although some considered the eighties to be TOTALLY AWESOME!

During this decade Wayne Williams was arrested in Atlanta for the murders of 23 black children; 52 hostages were released from their 444 days of captivity in Iran; the Vietnam Veterans Memorial, inscribed with 58,220 names of American soldiers killed or missing in Vietnam, was dedicated; Ivan Boesky of Drexel Burnham Lambert made headlines with insider trading scandals, Geraldine Ferraro was the first female presidential candidate, Jesse Jackson was the first black candidate for democrat Presidential nomination, the sexual revolution encountered a major adversary when Rock Hudson died of AIDS; the stock market tripled in 7 years yet survived the 1987 crash; televangelist Jim Bakker was sentenced to 45 years for federal charges of mail and wire fraud and of conspiring to defraud the public. Prisons overflowed, and violent crime rates, which, in 1980, had tripled since 1960, continued to climb with the appearance of crack cocaine in 1985. From 1985 to 1990 the use of cocaine addiction was up 35 percent, though the number of users had declined. Nancy Reagan's "Just Say No" campaign had great influence.

During this decade life became more stressful as there were two recessions. Divorce rates were increasing as this was accepted, as women had more rights. There was a growing proportion of split-parent families. Moreover, families led increasingly busier lives; the increase of working mothers saw a fundamental change in activities for some families. With both parents at work, there was less time for the children and family time. In particular, people's lifestyle was busier and, like the 1970s, there was a lot more choice. With many restaurants nearby and ready made meals introduced foods such as Pot Noodle Casserole became increasingly popular. Life was starting to become more convenient for single parents and working parents. Cooking and cleaning were not a priority, and the introduction of the time saving small appliances, such as the microwave were also convenient for the working mother. Families changed drastically during these years. The 80s continued the trends of the 60s and 70s - more divorces, more unmarried couples living together, more single parent families. The two-earner family was even more common than in previous decades, more women earned college and advanced degrees, married, and had fewer children.

THE 1990S - THE POST-COLD WAR DECADE

The 1990s was truly the electronic age. The World Wide Web was born in 1992, changing the way we communicate and spend our money. Online shopping, online gambling and e-commerce were introduced. In 1989, 15% of American households had a computer; by 2000, this figure had increased to 51%.

According to Pew Research, Fact Tank: May 25, 2017, 90% of U.S. households contained at least one of these devices: smartphone, desktop/laptop computer, tablet, or streaming media device, with the typical American household containing five of them. And nearly one-in-five American households 18% were "hyper-connected" – meaning they contained 10 or more of these devices.

What were the effects of social media on our society? The 90s was a decade of enormous disruption, the axis on which the old world ended and a new one began.

Speaking of those who lived through some of its most compelling moments, Senator Marco Rubio of Florida said, "That period of the '90s from the fall of the Berlin Wall to 9/11 was one of extraordinary transformation societally, economically and in our politics. A lot of the roots of the things we are facing today came from that period."

Next up came the world's first televised war—one that was broadcast in real time, on a 24-hour news cycle. CNN reporters embedded in Baghdad and on the Kuwaiti border were providing the White House with more information than it was getting from its own generals.

Bill Clinton appeared on "The Arsenio Hall Show," and instead of speaking policy, he played his saxophone. Everything changed. Yeah, he smoked pot (but he didn't inhale). MTV became a legitimate media outlet for his messages and Generation X and the Baby Boomers got it. The World War II generation didn't—but they no longer mattered.

The 60s sexual revolution paled to the revolution of the 90s. Gay rights movement would eventually lead to a Supreme Court ruling making and same sex marriage legal in all 50 states. This was just another blow to morality.

THE MORAL DECLINE OF AMERICA - SPINNII
OUT-OF-CONTROL

Politics was also experiencing its own disruption: The Florida recount in the 2000 Bush–Gore presidential deadlock defined how divided a nation America had become. But it also had an even more pernicious effect. Days of uncertainty revolving around the unlikely "hanging chads" stalled a resolution. The election mechanisms—yet another institution—had failed.

The Supreme Court was called in to decide, divisively overruling the recount. This threw into doubt any idea that the system was one of fairness and justice, forcing both sides to entrench themselves further.

Over the past few decades, morals have changed; Churches have changed; Societies have changed; People have changed; But God's Word remains the same.

Romans 1:26-32: "Because of this, God gave them over to shameful lusts. Even their women exchanged natural sexual relations for unnatural ones. In the same way the men also abandoned natural relations with women and were inflamed with lust for one another. Men committed shameful acts with other men and received in themselves the due penalty for their error. Furthermore, just as they did not think it worthwhile to retain the knowledge of God, so God gave them over to a depraved mind, so that they do what ought not to be done. They have become filled with every kind of wickedness, evil, greed and depravity. They are full of envy, murder, strife, deceit, and malice. They are gossips, slanderers, God-haters, insolent, arrogant and boastful; they invent ways of doing evil; they disobey their parents; they have no understanding, no fidelity, no love, no mercy. Although they know God's righteous decree that those who do such things deserve death, they not only continue to do these very things but also approve of those who practice them."

This is a topic where you will either unwaveringly agree with me, or you will fervently disagree with me. I believe that the deterioration of family values began in 1941 when women were encouraged to join the work force, to replace the men who went to war.

After the war, many women faced problems when their jobs were given to male veterans who were returning to the work force. Women who were able to remain in the workforce were transferred back to "female" jobs which paid lesser wages.

The loss of jobs and the disparity of wages for women contributed to driving the wedge of resentment between men and women in the workplace. That war of equal pay for equal job responsibility is still being fought today.

Since the end of World War II, there has been a gradual deterioration of family values and a breakdown of the family unit, a trend where a mother was not at home to take care of her children, monitor their behavior, help with the homework and discipline when and where necessary. The two-parent family structure has all but disappeared in a society where both parents are absent from the home for the majority of the waking hours of the children.

I have to say that we should admire the women, the "stay at home mothers" who may have sacrificed their dreams of a career. To them, the importance of raising their children, nurturing, and loving them meant more to them than a job or a career. I realize there are women who have no choice but to work; let's not forget them. The main point is that the nuclear family structure has suffered and continues to suffer for many reasons.

In many cases there is no one to teach children the importance of respect and ethical behavior. The once important family time at the dinner table has given way to processed, packaged meals prepared in a microwave and fast food, eaten on the fly. Many parents no longer focus on probing into how their children's day went, asking important questions about their friends, interests, and schoolwork. Dinner table discussions are mostly a thing of the past. In many homes there is no longer family prayer before the meal...All of this has gone by the wayside. In many homes, children retreat to their bedrooms and lose themselves in video games and social media. They spend endless hours unmonitored and isolated from seemingly uncaring, uninterested parents.

Don't get me wrong; I know there are families out there where family time and dinner table conversation and interaction are still an important part of their lives. For these families, it becomes more and more difficult for the intimate family nucleus to exist as once was common. Peer pressures on the children of households where a strong family core exists encourage the children to rebel, wanting to be like their friends who have many freedoms because of absentee parents. The more these children strive for independence and individuality, the more they are transformed by the world. Hence, there is undue tension in the household, and all too often the parents give in to the outside pressures of society.

The advancement in technology has also harmed family values. Social media and television, as well as instant access to potentially harmful information, contribute to the decline of values in our society. This has led to a lack of discipline and an overt disregard for authority on the part of many young people. So as to not be a hypocrite, I must also point out that an alarming percentage of adults who are old enough to know better show the same lack of discipline and disregard for authority. Who can children look to as role models?

One example alone is that 50 years ago a teacher was happy to go to school to teach; a teacher was respected and looked up to; a teacher could discipline if necessary. Today many teachers fear for their lives; they are afraid of their students. Discipline by teachers and parents alike is restricted in some cases. It appears there is no longer a healthy fear of chastisement, and self-control has gone out the door.

I don't know about you, but when I was a kid in school, teachers were permitted to discipline me and if I got in trouble at school, the discipline at school paled in comparison to the discipline I would receive at home.

In many school districts across the country education has evolved into the Critical Race Theory or (CRT) which is an intellectual movement holding beliefs that racial bias is inherent in many parts of western society, especially in its legal and social institutions, on the basis that they have been primarily designed for and implemented by white people. Additionally, the "Inclusive and Diversity" movement introduces other challenges, such as the removal of pronouns related to gender. It is so sad to see our country going down many wrong roads. Christian values and God have been replaced by a homosexual/transgender empathetic agenda, and God's promise, the rainbow, has been hijacked by leftists and elitist politics.

This blatant lack of respect carries over to other social interactions of society today. Is it too late? Who can we look to? We can look to God our Creator. What does

God's Word tell us? "Whoever spares the rod hates their children, but the one who loves his/her children is diligent to discipline them." (Proverbs 13:24)

This Scripture does not call for us to beat our children. It does, however, tell us that children need to be disciplined when necessary. Discipline, to be effective, must be administered impartially and consistently. In other words, negative behaviors need to be dealt with each and every time and not allowed to go unaddressed, which may lead to an explosive situation that ends with both parent and child angry and possibly out of control. Children need to know their boundaries. They will test those boundaries from time to time, and they need to know that violations will be dealt with every time they cross the line.

You may notice that many families who have immigrated from other countries have strong family values, traditions, respect, and their children often excel in their studies. The parents have impressed on their children that their education is more important than their popularity at school. They teach their children that good study habits lead to good grades, hence there is less face time with video games, social media, and television. These responsible parents see to it that their children are *not* influenced by our overly liberal society.

I have some dear missionary friends whose children were raised in a foreign country. These friends came to the U.S. on furlough, and after their children attended public school for some time, they noticed the influences of peer pressure. Their children were no longer living in the protected environment they had grown up in. Even though the family values had not changed, the children were beginning to show signs of the negative influences of our liberal society.

Our friends felt it was important that they should put their children into a private parochial school, to shield them from the undue influences they were being exposed to in the liberal public school system. Praise the Lord, the parents saw the problem before a wedge had been driven between parent and child.

I believe it is Satan's number one goal to drive that wedge between parent and child. The devil seeks to weaken and ultimately destroy the family unit. Satan is at work 24/7. Look around you; I believe you cannot deny my assertion evidenced by the continued moral decline of our society.

I can point to some strong evidence to support my words. The following are just a few:

On January 22, 1973, the United States Supreme Court, in a 7-2 decision, handed down two rulings legalizing abortion in America. According to the National Right to Life Committee, since that time an estimated 64 million unborn babies have been killed, yet the United States still permitted the continued abortion of babies, with no end in sight. UPDATE: June 24, 2022, the Supreme Court in a 5-4 decision overturned Roe V. Wade, the landmark ruling that established the constitutional right to abortion. Immediately protesters took to the streets and civil disobedience wracked the country. Some states upheld their laws to allow abortion, others followed the Supreme Court's decision.

Marijuana is legal in many states, treated the same way that alcohol is treated under the law: adults over 21 are permitted to possess, grow, and smoke or in other ways, ingest marijuana.

A stunning new poll has revealed that just 1 in 3 members of one of the largest Protestant denominations in the

United States believes that Jesus Christ is the only way to salvation.

Same sex marriage is legal in all 50 states.

Believe it or not the topsy-turvy laws of today restrict parents on how they can discipline their children. A child of fifty years ago would never have dreamed of treating their parents the way some children disrespect their parents today.

Yes, abuse needs to be checked and prevented, but at the same time, discipline, or the fear of it begets respect. We all want to see in our children, examples of honesty, integrity, and respect for others as well as for self. We, as parents, need to provide a positive role model for our children.

Are we Americans, we the people, proud enough and patriotic enough to protect and defend our family values? Are we as Americans bold enough to stand up and fight for honesty and integrity; to speak out against the wrongs we see in today's society and in our government? Are we courageous enough to declare that Jesus is Lord, and take back from Satan the values we once held dear?

Only God can turn this world around. We have the power to choose. Do we take the road that leads to eternal damnation, or do we choose the narrow road that leads to the glory of the Lord?

DANGERS OF THE DIGITAL WORLD

In an increasingly digital world, most people own multiple electronic devices with screens. However, many parents worry about the effects of screen use on themselves and their children.

With screens virtually everywhere, controlling a child's screen time can be challenging. How can you manage your children's screen time? How will you know if you or your children are addicted to screens or video games?

It's difficult to avoid screens completely, especially with their importance at work and school. However, excessive screen time can affect a person's mental, social and physical health.

Children are more vulnerable than ever to predatory grooming via portable multimedia devices. As with most things in life, it usually comes down to moderation. Too much time spent on social media, video games, etc., etc. is unhealthy. We live in a world of confusion where truth has degraded to a virtual reality. The worldview of truth can be whatever fits the situation. God is our moral compass and our absolute truth.

NEGATIVE EFFECTS OF SOCIAL MEDIA

1: Unreal expectations

2: Loneliness and isolation

3: Sleep issues

4: Mood swings

5: Self-absorption

6: Relationship issues

7: Influence eating habits

8: Social media addiction

9: Depression and sadness

POSITIVE EFFECTS OF SOCIAL MEDIA

1: Find almost anyone and any thing

2: Connect with people

3: Share a common challenge/interest

4: Access to information

5: Motivation and inspiration

God loves His people, we are the chosen, the elect. We are also prodigals, and He waits on us. He is a jealous God, He will shower us with goodness, without restraint. We, as a people, must cry out to God and turn our faces back to Him.

CHAPTER 4

Has Our Society Been Hijacked?

"American Society Hijacked" could be a political slogan for almost any party or group within the United States at the moment. It does not depend on your beliefs; it is equally appropriate to all parties, cults, fanatics, normal people and, certainly, to every politician.

What is hijacking? The encyclopedia says hijacking is, "an act of unlawfully seizing an aircraft, vehicle, or ship while in transit. Hijacking is a felony crime where a person uses force, or the threat of force, to seize control of an occupied transport vessel such as an airplane or motor vehicle for the purposes of taking possession of it or the valuable goods contained by the vessel.

How does hijacking peoples minds work?

I do not believe "society" hijacks the minds of people. In fact, everybody likes to blame "society" for things because they do not know who to blame, so I try to avoid the use of that term. Even though I point to society in my writings, I cannot always blame society. We individuals have allowed the evils of this world to creep into our everyday lives. We, collectively, are responsible! It's just too easy to place blame on something or someone other than ourselves. Aren't you part of society? Am I not part of society?

America and all of Christendom! We stand at the threshold! What will we do? What will you do? Are you willing to read on and take steps to preserve what the All-Mighty God has blessed? Or are you going to sit back while our nation unravels? We need to take a stand, but first, we need to drop to our knees and ask God to offer us once again, as a people and as a nation, His Grace. Grace is unmerited, undeserved favor, something we are in great need of NOW!

The reality is our nation is exceedingly divided. We are an immensely wealthy, militarized, ethnically, and culturally divided nation.

America's bankers, corporations and über -wealthy are deemed "too big to fail" and have unquestioningly been let off the hook to pay their fair share. We the people have stood by silently and handed them the keys to the country to remove jobs and rights from citizens, workers, and homeowners. We have gone along while our federal government bailed them out to the tune of tens of billions of taxpayer dollars. The United States as a nation, like the USSR before it, has allowed its government to be hijacked by lobbyists and big money. Our once praised political system seems to be hopelessly paralyzed and it appears our government at all levels has become "too big to succeed."

Since when have we Americans had no other choice than settling ever year for less and less as the U.S. becomes more and more third world by default? The U.S. economy is rapidly being overtaken in the world economy. Countries such as China and India are at the threshold of entering as "first world" nations.

The American public is disillusioned with our government and its hypocrisy. It seems that, in general, we the people have lost the ability to think for ourselves. Has the helpless passivity of our country replaced the American "can do" attitude of the 1950s?

Make no mistake about it: the American economy is in the throes of the longest, most protracted recovery since the Great Depression. Our people and our government should be focused on fixing our tattered economy.

While I cannot disagree that fixing the financial system is a critical factor in restoring our standing in the global economy and that getting people back to work will solve many of our problems, I would challenge our government and those who actually care about our country to take a long hard look at one of the key underlying causes of the disintegration of our nation. Government's unrestricted hand-outs of trillions of dollars into our economy have had an adverse impact on people who are unwilling to go back to work.

If there's a problem with people's minds being "hijacked" I'm afraid, you'll need to ask some more searching questions than just blaming "society".

How about asking yourself *why* a mind that doesn't want to be "hijacked" can be hijacked? Why is it that people *allow* their minds to be in such a weakened state? It is the proverbial "frog in the pot of water." People are allowing themselves to literally get snowed over. On the other hand, they resist quickly enough if they recognize that someone is trying to deceive them.

The premise of hijacking is that it undermines your control. This system is better at hijacking your instincts than you are at controlling them. You'd have to exert an enormous amount of energy to control whether or not these things are manipulating you all the time.

TECHNOLOGY, IS IT HIJACKING PEOPLE IN WAYS WE DON'T, SEE?

There's an invisible problem that's affecting all of society. There is an overabundance of social media platforms that people of all ages have access to. Facebook, Twitter, Instagram, Snapchat, TikTok, YouTube, and Google, to name a few, have produced amazing products that have benefited the world enormously. But these companies are caught in a zero-sum race for our finite attention, which they need to make money. Constantly forced to outperform their competitors, they must use increasingly persuasive techniques to keep us glued. They point artificial intelligence-driven news feeds, content, and notifications at our minds, continually learning how to hook us more deeply. These parasitic social media platforms are especially motivated, to enrich the lives of their creators and the staff that supports them.

UNFORTUNATELY, WHAT IS BEST FOR CAPTURING OUR ATTENTION IS NOT BEST FOR OUR WELL-BEING:

- Snapchat turns conversations into streaks, redefining how our children measure friendship.
- Instagram glorifies the picture-perfect life, eroding our physical self-worth.
- Facebook segregates us into echo chambers, fragmenting our communities.

- YouTube auto plays the next video within seconds, even if it eats into our sleep.

These are not neutral products. They are part of a predatory system designed to addict us, and it appears to be working.

These platforms or technologies are in effect, destructive and voracious, with the sole purpose of seizing control of your mind, your time, your life. Time is finite. Time is something we cannot add to or accumulate more of. These platforms also track your location, your spending habits, and what occupies your time viewing while logged into social media. Suddenly advertisements pop up on your computer screen or the inbox of your email. Take TikTok for instance, a social media platform that is exceedingly popular with young people. TikTok is a platform aimed at wasting your time and introducing you to information and images that typically you would not allow yourself to view. It is a time thief and a mind polluter. My intention is not to declare TikTok as the "Lone Waster of Time" most social media platforms become addictive and rob us of valuable, productive time.

We must be on guard, for Satan knows exactly how to use predaceous technology to destroy lives. Be diligent in limiting time on computers and cell phones with your children as well as yourselves. Turn-off location trackers on your cell phone and on your child's cell phone.

Learn to use social media responsibly, or do not use it at all, the choice is yours. Teach your children to use social media responsibly and set limits. Children and teenagers included, should be encouraged to avoid access to computers and cell phones behind closed doors, the temptations are too great. Set household rules that state that access to social media must have a daily time limit with no exceptions.

ARE RADICAL ACTIVISTS TRANSFORMING OUR COMMUNITIES?

Our communities that once preached love and acceptance of others have been hijacked by radical activists who continue to push extreme concepts onto society. They have in the past targeted collegiate academia to poison the minds of our college-age young adults, and in recent years are specifically targeting elementary school-age children. They hide among the teacher unions, our community boards of education, our educators, and the corporations that produce the curriculum to poison the minds of our children who are, in many cases, being taught by teachers whose minds have been jaded by the collegiate educational systems. This, my friends, is a well-planned satanic attack on our society. And, unbelievably, this has crept up on us. The Covid pandemic has helped to open the eyes of parents and well-meaning teachers who are at the mercy of the school boards and greed driven politicians.

There is a growing trend among anti-elitist politicians and community leaders who consider themselves to be superior in intellect, talent, power, wealth, and/or position in society. There is always something disingenuous about anti-elitist politics. Plenty of investment bankers are Democrat, and Republican politicians who claim to speak for devoutly religious cultural conservatives are usually far removed from the world (and the values) of those whose votes they court and whose resentments they stoke. Nothing more exposes the hypocrisy of financial elites, riding the coattails of those who revere small-town religious values, than a downturn that highlights the vast gulf in power between the two key components of the conservative coalition. Even cultural conservatives will start to notice that taxing policies are geared toward the wealthy investing class, not toward the paycheck crowd. This political behavior further drives the wedge between the "haves" and the "have-nots." Divide and conquer is a tool of the evil one. Unity in the body of Christ can and will overcome the evildoers, if only we, as a nation, will turn our faces back to the Lord our God and rely on Him as our Founding Fathers did. It was their intent that we as a nation, trust in our Creator and prayerfully consider our Judeo-Christian roots in governance and critical evaluation of guiding our country and its citizens in manners pleasing to God.

They are the anti-elitest politicians and cultural conservative community leaders who indeed, have a satanic inclination to be forever in charge – to control the machinery of government however undemocratic – in order to use the resources of the state in consolidating their greed for power on the unsuspecting masses as they remain continuously in a state of poverty and dependency on government.

THE CANCEL CULTURE

Cancel culture, also known as the call-out culture, is a fashionable phrase of the late 2010s and early 2020s used to refer to a culture in which those who are deemed to have acted or spoken in an unacceptable manner are ostracized, boycotted, or shunned.

The Cancel Culture is a collective attempt to harm the reputation, livelihood, and social presence of people, corporations, products, TV shows, celebrities, employees, etc., for violating a particular ideological standard.

Cancel Culture is a form of social media mob rule. Conservative politicians and pundits have increasingly embraced the argument that cancel culture rather than being a way of speaking truth to power has spun out of control and become a senseless form of social mob rule.

If you challenge their position or ideology on any given topic, their tactics include, but are not limited to, shouting you down, campaigning against your position, or escalating to the point of personal property destruction and even bodily harm. They know no boundaries to shutting you down.

CHAPTER 5

Decline & Fall of the American Empire

Despite the aura of omnipotence most empires project, a look at their history should remind us that they are/were fragile societies. So delicate is their ecology of power that, when things start to go truly bad, empires regularly unravel at unholy speed: just a year for Portugal, two years for the Soviet Union, eight years for France, 11 years for the Ottomans, 17 years for Great Britain, and, in all likelihood, 22 years for the United States, counting from the crucial year 2003.

May 1 – U.S. President George W. Bush lands on the aircraft carrier USS Abraham Lincoln, where he gives a speech announcing the end of major combat in the 2003 Invasion of Iraq. A banner behind him declares "Mission Accomplished".

Future historians are likely to identify the Bush administration's rash invasion of Iraq in that year as the start of America's downfall. However, instead of the bloodshed that marked the end of so many past empires, with cities burning and civilians slaughtered, this twenty-first century imperial collapse could come relatively quietly through the invisible tendrils of economic collapse or cyberwarfare.

But have no doubt: when Washington's global dominion finally ends, there will be painful daily reminders of what such a loss of power means for Americans in every walk of life. As a half-dozen European nations have discovered, imperial decline tends to have a remarkably demoralizing impact on a society, regularly bringing at least a generation of economic privation. As the economy cools, political temperatures rise, often sparking serious domestic unrest. The West needs a revival, or we are doomed to failure just as past empires have experienced.

Now it's America's turn. The United States is going to collapse. This isn't a fear-mongering statement. Just a fact and our economists know it.

Whether in two years or fifty, the days of America-as-global-superpower are numbered.

Our democracy, our way of life, could flip upside down, becoming similar to what is depicted in the George Orwell Sci-Fi novel, 1984. Our country becomes a dystopian, totalitarian superstate, under the constant surveillance of the thought police. Big Brother is everywhere, but never appears publicly but instead appears only on propaganda posters, advertising billboards, and television monitors. Does it sound impossible?

As our downward spiral accelerates you will see US Global military bases being turned over to foreign governments. Our government, in order to make a last-ditch effort to enslave its own people in a "soft-totalitarian panopticon state," (under constant surveillance). Our currency will be replaced by Bitcoin or a similar virtual currency. It is coming and we *must* resist the continued surveillance and the virtual currencies. It will not be easy, but our freedom, our very lives, depend on it.

For those familiar with *the mark of the beast – 666,* none are completely certain what exactly that means, but virtual currency is likely to be in play during the 7-year tribulation. Let me call your attention to the last book of the Bible, the book of Revelation. The mark of the beast is *the mark of mankind.* It is the opposite of the divine plan of salvation. Revelation, chapters 16:2 and 19:20 cite the "mark of the beast" as a sign that identifies those who worship the beast out of the sea (Rev. 13:1). This beast is identified as the antichrist. This mark is first mentioned in (Rev. 13:16-17), where it is imposed on humanity by the beast out of the earth (Rev.13:11). This second beast is the false prophet (Rev. 19:20), who forces the worship of the antichrist and brands those who do so with the mark. This mark is equivalent to the beast's name or number (Rev. 13:17; cf. Rev.14:11). This mysterious and unknowable number is announced in (Rev.13:18) as 666, the mark of the beast is taken by those who value personal safety over fidelity to Christ.

The bottom line to all of the following (which I have not researched and intend to dismiss with less specificity to numbers, speculation, and such.) Without world and economic analysts to back my assertions; I predict the downfall and subsequent unraveling of our existence as a nation is a result to our turning our backs, as a society and nation, on our Creator.

AND THEN IT WILL COLLAPSE

According to **The Nation:** The oldest continuously published weekly magazine in the United States, covering progressive political and cultural news, opinion, and analysis.

Their 2010 edition predicted the following: The U.S. has already reached a point where it's no longer the dominant global power, with its share of the global economy getting smaller.

Fast forward a decade, Gross Domestic Product (GDP) numbers have been updated from the 2010 predictions.

According to the US Bureau of Economic Analysis, the U.S. portion of the global Gross Domestic Product (GDP) has declined from 35%, 3rd quarter 2020 to just 3%, 3rd quarter 2022. America's economic role is not even a quarter of what it used to be. By 2030, China will jump ahead and become the world's preeminent economic superpower.

Some economists have predicted a soft landing and America's demise to be somewhere between 2040 and 2050.

Don't bet on it. The demise of the United States as the global superpower could come far more quickly than anyone imagines. If Washington is dreaming of 2040 or 2050 as the end of the American Century, a more realistic assessment of domestic and global trends suggests that in 2025, just 2 short years from now, it could all be over except for the shouting. If that doesn't grab your attention, I am not sure what could.

It is a sobering accusation. I am not sure when it will come, but it will come because we, as a nation, have turned our backs on our Creator. History will repeat itself, just as it did with the nation of Israel centuries ago, they also turned their backs on God, which led to their destruction and exile by pagan nations.

Available economic, educational, and military data indicate that, when it comes to US global power, negative trends have aggregated rapidly since 2020 and are likely to reach a critical mass no later than 2030. The American Century, proclaimed so triumphantly at the start of World War II, will be tattered, and fading by 2025, its eighth decade, "Favored Nation, founded on the Divine Providence of God" could likely be history by 2030.

Significantly, in 2008, the US National Intelligence Council admitted for the first time that America's global power was indeed on a declining trajectory. In one of its periodic futuristic reports, Global Trends 2025, the Council cited "the transfer of global wealth and economic power now under way, roughly from West to East" and "without precedent in modern history," as the primary factor in the decline of the "United States' relative strength—even in the military realm." Like many in Washington, however, the Council's analysts anticipated a very long, very soft landing for American global preeminence, and harbored the hope that somehow the US would long "retain unique military capabilities, to project military power globally" for decades to come.

No such luck. Under current projections, the United States will find itself in second place behind China (already the world's second largest economy) in economic output around 2025. Similarly, Chinese innovation is on a trajectory toward world leadership in applied science and military technology, just as America's current supply of brilliant scientists and engineers retires, without adequate replacement by an ill-educated younger generation.

By 2025, according to projected plans, the Pentagon will throw a military "Hail Mary" pass for a dying empire. It will launch a lethal triple canopy of advanced aerospace robotics that represents Washington's last best hope of retaining global power despite its waning economic influence. By that year, however, China's global network of communications satellites, backed by the world's most powerful supercomputers, will also be fully operational, providing Beijing with an independent platform for the weaponization of space and a powerful communications system for missile or cyber-strikes into every quadrant of the globe.

Wrapped in imperialistic arrogance, like Briton's Whitehall before it, the White House still seems to imagine that American decline will be gradual, gentle, and partial. In his State of the Union address January 2010, President Obama offered the reassurance that "I do not accept second place for the United States of America." A few days later, Vice (now President) President Biden ridiculed the very idea that "we are destined to fulfill historian Paul Kennedy's prophecy that we are going to be a great nation that has failed because we lost control of our economy and overextended."

Viewed historically, the question is not whether the United States will lose its unchallenged global power, but just how precipitous and wrenching the decline will be.

ECONOMIC DECLINE: PRESENT SITUATION

Today, three main threats exist to America's dominant position in the global economy: loss of economic clout thanks to a shrinking share of world trade, the decline of American technological innovation, and the end of the dollar's privileged status as the global reserve currency.

By 2008, the United States had already fallen to number three in global merchandise exports, with just 11% of them compared to 12% for China and 16% for the European Union. There is no reason to believe that this trend will reverse itself.

Similarly, American leadership in technological innovation is on the wane. After leading the world for decades in 25- to 34-year-olds with university degrees, the country sank to 12th place in 2010. The World Economic Forum ranked the United States at a mediocre 52nd among 139 nations in the quality of its university math and science instruction in 2010. Nearly half of all graduate students in the sciences in the US are now foreigners, most of whom will be heading home, not staying here as they once would have. By 2025, in other words, the United States is likely to face a critical shortage of talented scientists.

ECONOMIC DECLINE: SCENARIO 2020

After years of swelling deficits fed by incessant warfare in distant lands, in 2020, as long expected, the US dollar finally lost its special status as the world's reserve currency. Suddenly, the cost of imports soars. Unable to pay for swelling deficits by selling now-devalued Treasury notes abroad, Washington is finally forced to slash its bloated military budget. Under pressure at home and abroad, Washington slowly pulls US forces back from hundreds of overseas bases to a continental perimeter. By now, however, it is far too late.

Faced with a fading superpower incapable of paying the bills, China, India, Iran, Russia, and other powers, great and regional, provocatively challenge US dominion over the oceans, space, and cyberspace. Meanwhile, amid soaring prices, ever-rising unemployment, and a continuing decline in real wages, domestic divisions widen into violent clashes and divisive debates, often over remarkably irrelevant issues. Riding a political tide of disillusionment and despair, a far-right patriot, Donald Trump captures the presidency with thundering rhetoric, demanding respect for American authority and threatening military retaliation or economic reprisal. The world pays next to no attention as the American Century ends in silence.

Oil Shock: Present Situation, President Biden's debacle, America's waning economic power has been its lock on global oil supplies. Speeding by America's gas-guzzling economy in the passing lane, China became the world's number one energy consumer, a position the US had held for over a century. Energy specialists have argued that this change means China will "set the pace in shaping our global future."

By 2025, Iran and Russia will control almost half of the world's natural gas supply, which will potentially give them enormous leverage over energy-starved Europe. Add petroleum reserves to the mix and, as the National Intelligence Council has warned, in just 15 years two countries, Russia and Iran, could "emerge as energy kingpins."

Unless this speeding train is turned around the United States will remain so dependent upon foreign oil that a few adverse developments in the global energy market in 2025 spark an oil shock. Currently oil price shocks have quadrupled the cost of oil-based products and it will continue to get worse unless the current administration admits to the debacle and opens the pipelines and resumes oil production.

Within a few years, the US could be functionally bankrupt, and the clock is ticking toward midnight on the American Century.

MILITARY MISADVENTURE: PRESENT SITUATION

In the same way that Rome pulled back its troops from Alexandria in Egypt and the Scottish borders in Britain, the American military-industrial complex will continue to shrink. Its hasty withdrawal from Afghanistan, leaving an enormous cache of weapons, ammunition, artillery, rocket and missile defense systems, drones, aircraft, armored vehicles, trucks . . . the list is too enormous to be enumerated here, you get my drift, I am sure of it.

Counterintuitively, as their power wanes, empires often plunge into ill-advised military misadventures. This phenomenon is known among historians of empires as "micro-militarism" and seems to involve psychologically compensatory efforts to relieve the sting of retreat or defeat by occupying new territories, however briefly and catastrophically. These operations, irrational even from an imperial point of view, often yield hemorrhaging expenditures or humiliating defeats that only accelerate the loss of power.

STORMS OF CONFLICT

The following is currently "pure fiction", but it is not out of the question that, could occur, based on existing global tensions.

World War III: Scenario 2025

The technology of space and cyberwarfare is so new and untested that even the most outlandish scenarios may soon be superseded by a reality still hard to conceive. If we simply employ the sort of scenarios that the Air Force itself used in its 2009 "Future Capabilities Game", however, we can gain "a better understanding of how air, space and cyberspace overlap in warfare," and so begin to imagine how the next world war might actually be fought.

It's 11:59 p.m. on Thanksgiving Thursday in 2025. While cyber-shoppers pound the portals of Best Buy for deep discounts on the latest home electronics from China, US Air Force technicians at the Space Surveillance Telescope (SST) on Maui choke on their coffee as their panoramic screens suddenly blip to black. Thousands of miles away at the US Cybercommand's operation center in Texas, cyberwarriors soon detect malicious binaries that, though fired anonymously, show the distinctive digital fingerprints of China's People's Liberation Army.

The first overt strike is one nobody predicted. Chinese "malware" seizes control of the robotics aboard an unmanned solar-powered US Vulture Drone as it flies at 70,000 feet over the Tsushima Strait between Korea and Japan. It suddenly fires all the rocket pods beneath its enormous 400-foot wingspan, sending dozens of lethal missiles plunging harmlessly into the Yellow Sea, effectively disarming this formidable weapon.

Determined to fight fire with fire, the White House authorizes a retaliatory strike. Confident that its F-6 "Fractionated, Free-Flying" satellite system is impenetrable, Air Force commanders in California transmit robotic codes to the flotilla of X-37B space drones orbiting 250 miles above the Earth, ordering them to launch their "Triple Terminator" missiles at China's 35 satellites. Zero response. In near panic, the Air Force launches its Falcon Hypersonic Cruise Vehicle into an arc 100 miles above the Pacific Ocean and then, just 20 minutes later, sends the computer codes to fire missiles at seven Chinese satellites in nearby orbits. The launch codes are suddenly inoperative.

As the Chinese virus spreads uncontrollably through the F-6 satellite architecture, while those second-rate US supercomputers fail to crack the malware's devilishly complex code, GPS signals crucial to the navigation of US ships and aircraft worldwide are compromised. Carrier fleets begin steaming in circles in the mid-Pacific. Fighter squadrons are grounded. Reaper drones fly aimlessly toward the horizon, crashing when their fuel is exhausted. Suddenly, the United States loses what the US Air Force has long called "the ultimate high ground:" space. Within hours, the military power that had dominated the globe for nearly a century has been defeated in World War III without a single human casualty.

A New World Order?

Even if future events prove duller than these four scenarios suggest, every significant trend points toward a far more striking decline in American global power by 2025 than anything Washington now seems to be envisioning.

As allies worldwide begin to realign their policies to take cognizance of rising Asian powers, the cost of maintaining more than 1000 military bases and/or military installations. These bases/installations are spread over 63 countries. These overseas military bases will simply become unsustainable, finally forcing a staged withdrawal on a still-unwilling Washington. With both the US and China in a race to weaponize space and cyberspace, tensions between the two powers are bound to rise, making military conflict by 2025 at least feasible, if hardly guaranteed.

If America's decline is in fact on a 22-year trajectory from 2003 to 2025, then we have already frittered away most of the two decades of that decline with wars that distracted us from long-term problems and, like water tossed onto desert sands, wasted trillions of desperately needed dollars.

Endless scenarios could be concocted, but the point remains, that the US economy is shrinking and our influence on world politics is waning. The war between Ukraine and Russia, currently is severely impacting our military strength. Complicating matters even more, the economic, military, and technological trends outlined above will not operate in tidy isolation. As happened to European empires after World War II, such negative forces will undoubtedly prove synergistic. They will combine in thoroughly unexpected ways, create crises for which Americans are remarkably unprepared, and threaten to spin the economy into a sudden downward spiral, consigning this country to a generation or more of economic misery.

CHAPTER 6

Fences and Boundaries

We were created with a passion to live. To be indifferent to what is within us is literally to be without passion. God's solution to restraining our passions is His commands. Paradoxically, the Scriptures place human desires and passions at the very core of human action. Paul illustrates this passion transformation in Galatians 5:24: "Those who belong to Christ Jesus have crucified the sinful nature with its passions and desires." The Scriptures have a completely different view of human desire and passion. Rather than eliminate our passions, it is God's intention for us to overcome them with new passions. The compulsion of our passions becomes our character, and while sinful character burns hot for self-destructive passions that consume and destroy, the character of God ignites passion for what is good and true.

Our hearts crave the freedom of pleasure and the pleasure of freedom. But, there is something strangely elusive about freedom. When we were at last free, what actions and behaviors defined our freedom? Not all free acts lead to freedom. Sin creates the illusion of freedom. In the end it tricks us into seeking freedom from God rather than finding freedom in God.

Our society values youthfulness over wisdom and potential contributions by the elderly are often ignored. As Christians, we should reverse those values whenever we can. Encourage older people to share their wisdom and experience. Listen carefully when they speak. Offer them your friendship and help them to find ways to continue to serve God.

God in His wisdom has provided fences, walls, and boundaries for our well-being that we might not stray into terrain that destroys the very essence for which we were made. Our Creator has put those limits in place as a safeguard. Our poor judgment can sometimes do irreparable harm to us and to others. We tend to believe the greatest dangers to us come from others but, in reality, we are sometimes our own worst enemy. The boundaries are there to shelter us, principally from ourselves.

The social libertarian may find great ecstasy in the sound of their falling, but it may well be the very death knell of the one for whose protection the barriers were built. One of the most aberrant breeds in the American political scene these days is the one who gleefully describes himself or herself as a fiscal conservative but a social liberal. That is just another way of saying that people must live within their means financially but can die beyond their means socially.

Are You in Tune? A musical metaphor

Music has changed a great deal over the years; actually, it has drastically changed over the centuries. The musical notes have been the same, I assume, since mankind learned how to make music. Somewhere along the way, man was able to distinguish between the melodies musical instruments could make and the unrestrained noise they can make. It doesn't necessarily take a trained ear to distinguish between the two. I have to admit that some of the music of current times sounds like uncontrolled noise to me, but of course, the difference between melody and noise is somewhat determined by personal choice.

There are absolute rules for music, even the kinds that fall into the category I label as "noise." It is a widely accepted standard that many instruments are tuned using the note of "Middle-C" as a reference point. The term middle C is designated C_4 in scientific pitch notation because of the note's position as the fourth C key on a standard 88-key piano keyboard. In other words, in the world of music this rule is an "absolute." From the classically trained musician to the untrained, self-trained rock and roll musician, the rules of musical notes are absolute. The middle C of a well-tuned piano is the standard reference point for tuning many instruments.

When I was taking violin lessons, at the beginning of each session the teacher would have me tune my violin to her piano. Starting with A, the second highest string, it should match the pitch of A above the middle C of her piano. Next the D string should match the D just above the middle C of her piano, and so-on and so-forth.

Not much of today's popular music has a pleasing melody to me, and the lyrics are difficult to understand, at best. From what I *can* understand of today's lyrics, I am probably better off not hearing them clearly.

There are some "old standards" that we all know. Their popularity will last for perhaps generations, and many of the classical musical arrangements will remain popular for all time. Then there are the pop songs that have very little melodic value, and they will be forgotten almost as quickly as they became known.

Although musical tastes change over time musical notes are absolute. They remain the same yesterday, today, and tomorrow; in other words, they are an unchanging standard. The same is true of God; He is unchanging. God's Word is the absolute truth, and His Son Jesus is *our* "Middle C." Our lives remain in tune as long as we set our sights on Him and tune our lives to the character of Jesus.

An absolute truth, sometimes called a universal truth, is an unalterable and permanent fact. The concept of absolute truths - what they are and whether they exist - has been debated among many different groups of people. Philosophers have waded in the muck of defining absolute truth for millennia. For example, Plato believed that absolute truth existed, but that truth on earth was merely a shadow of great forms of absolute truth existing in the universe. Alternatively, many believe in relative truths, where facts may vary depending on the circumstances.

Absolute truth is something that is true at all times and in all places. It is something that is always true no matter what the circumstances. It is a fact that cannot be changed. For example, there are no round squares. There are also no square circles. The angles of a triangle add up to 180 degrees. These are all true by definition.

It's difficult to disprove the concept of absolute truth, since saying that there are no absolute truths - that it is absolutely true that no absolute truth exists - is itself an absolute truth. One can say, "From what I know, I believe there are no absolute truths." Still, this is murky territory.

Absolutes always, never changing, these are factors we depend on to guarantee the integrity of so many things in our world. Absolute measures of ingredients guarantee that a recipe will turn out as expected and make it pleasing to one's taste. Absolute architectural engineering methods guarantee the integrity of a building or structure. Absolute truth guarantees that expectations will be met. We sometimes say that things are absolutely true, or they are absolutely false. The musical notes, when arranged in a way that is pleasing to our ear, are beautiful and melodic, soothing for the soul. The same musical notes when arranged in a hap-hazard way are painful and displeasing to the ear.

Another danger we should beware of is that the devil can add a few grains of truth to what is false and make it sound as if it were true. Unless you are in tune with the Word of God you may fall victim to the "half-truth."

A NATION OBSESSED WITH REALITY

Are we a nation obsessed with reality or are we a nation obsessed with self-ruination? I read somewhere that rocker Tommy Lee once said, "We're not here for a long time, we're here for a good time." Moreover, the popular response from the era in which we live is, "Amen, Tommy." Many of the "Now Generation" follow his lead everyday by shunning the most basic principles of decent and clean living instead, trying to survive, and living reckless lifestyles. It appears, to me, there is nothing real about the reality shows created by many of our current TV and Hollywood moguls.

Once while waiting in an auto tire and repair shop, I was basically forced to watch a TV show that I had never heard of and that would never be broadcast into my living room unless it was a complete mistake. The show "Wendy Williams", which currently airs nationally in over 70% of the country, is a morning talk show where current events in the lives of celebrities are discussed: "Hot Topics" according to Wendy Williams. I don't know about you, but the lives of celebrities do not fall into any area of interest to me. I am only concerned about their lives in the way their public agendas affect the lives of impressionable young people, and gullible adults.

The rubbish I witnessed for the 35 minutes I had to wait for an oil change and tire rotation is NOT worthy of television airtime, but in this day and age it is considered entertainment. The audience appeared to be comprised entirely women in their early twenties to, perhaps their mid-thirties. Wendy Williams, the talk show host, started off by talking about a female celebrity who has recently gone through a divorce, in fact, it was her third divorce. Of late, this female celebrity has been frequently seen in public, with a much younger man. The question posed to the audience was: "Is it wrong for the celebrity to be out in public with another man so soon?" The talk show host said that this has been the "mantra" of this woman, and whether it is right or wrong for her to hop from man to man, and to be so public about it? In response the audience went wild, cheering for the celebrity, and applauding her life choices!

Is this what our younger generation looks up to? Have we, as a society, become so shallow that we think this kind of TV show is entertaining, *and* informative? I am sad to say that it appears we are there; a bunch of degenerates whose own lives are so boring that we spend our free time watching "reality" shows, mindless sit-coms, and talk shows where we live vicariously through the lives of celebrities *and* we seem to know more about their lives than the lives of our close relatives, and *even* our own children?

As Isaiah 59:12-15 says:

"For our offenses are many in your sight, and our sins testify against us. Our offenses are ever with us, and we acknowledge our iniquities: rebellion and treachery against the LORD, turning our backs on our God, inciting revolt and oppression, uttering lies our hearts have conceived. So justice is driven back, and righteousness stands at a distance; truth has stumbled in the streets, honesty cannot enter. Truth is nowhere to be found, and whoever shuns evil becomes a prey."

In the last chapter of his epistle the writer of the Hebrews is bringing everything he has said to a close. Near the middle of the chapter, he *writes* "Jesus Christ is the same yesterday, today and forever." (Hebrews 13:8) You could say that he was saying, "Jesus is and always will be our "middle C" and our lives are in tune only when tuned according to Him."

There are many sounds out there calling for us to tune our lives according to them. They ring out giving the impression that they will bring harmony and truth to our lives if only we will tune our lives to them. But we must not be deceived. Tuning one's life to anything or anyone other than Jesus leaves our lives flat, off key and out of harmony. Note the writer's stern warning following the grand proclamation about Jesus; "Do not be carried off by all kinds of strange teachings." (Hebrews13:9) Jesus alone is the middle C of all life. He is the Creator and sustainer of all things. He alone is the "I AM."

Because He is the same yesterday, today, and forever, our past, present, and future find forgiveness, cleansing, healing, and transformation in Him. He re-creates us and makes us new. He tunes our lives to Himself so that we resonate His presence and Person. Whenever life taps us, we resound Him. Once tuned to Him we must, by His grace and empowerment, keep ourselves tuned to Him. We listen to Him and His Word and lovingly obey, bringing every part of who we are and what we do into harmony with Him. It is more than asking "What would Jesus do?" and attempting to act as He would. It is having Jesus do it, in and through us. It is being so in tune with Him that our lives radiate and resemble Him.

Paul told the Philippian church that He is confident that the work Jesus has begun in them He will carry on to completion. Let us remain submitted and committed to Christ Jesus being confident that He will continue to bring our lives in tune with Him, making us more and more like Him - our Middle C.

WISDOM IS A GIFT FROM GOD

Knowing it all is one thing; knowing the One who truly does know it all is another.

We've all experienced the type of character who has an answer for everything, a smug summation even without being asked...

Then there's another type that's unfortunately rather rare: the person who drops pearls of true wisdom, the one with just the right thing to say at just the right moment, bringing just the right effect.

Do you ever wonder how they do it? Our human brains tell us that minds like that are either something we're born with or something we have to work at. James, however, tells us just the opposite. According to him, true wisdom, the kind that comes from heaven, is not about selfish ambition or boastfulness, but about living at the foot of our heavenly Father, passing on the things we hear in prayer and read in the Bible.

According to James 3:17, "But the wisdom that is from above is first pure, then peaceable, gentle, willing to yield, full of mercy and good fruits, without partiality and without hypocrisy." The Message translation takes it a few steps further: "Real wisdom, God's wisdom, begins with a holy life and is characterized by getting along with others. It is gentle and reasonable, overflowing with mercy and blessings, not hot one day and cold the next, not two-faced. You can develop a healthy, robust community that lives right with God and enjoy its results only if you do the hard work of getting along with each other, treating each other with dignity and honor." (3:17-18)

Think of it this way: without a dose of humility, getting along with others can be pretty difficult.

Now, in terms of teens and young adults—those who are still in the process of learning how to assert themselves and finding the bravado to carry them through their moments of insecurity—this can be a deep-down, life-changing, completely encouraging concept. With the words of James spurring them on, they can take the pressure off themselves to have all the answers. As humans, that's not really our job. Our role is to be a little slower to speak, a little more ready to listen. The fewer words we use, after all, the more weight those words will carry.

Scripture offers hope to those with an inflated sense of entitlement. For those who believe they are entitled to cell phones, computers, cars, and alcohol even if it is illegal, young people whose parents threaten to sue the authorities when the behavior of their teen is exposed.

It is amazing that God set before the Israelites a choice between blessings and curses. It is even more amazing that most of them, through their disobedience, chose curses. We have the same fundamental choices today. We can live for ourselves, or we can live in service to God. To choose our own way is to travel on a dead-end road, but to choose God's way is to receive eternal life. God's Word tells us in John 5:24 "I tell you the truth, whoever hears my word and believes him who sent me has eternal life and will not be condemned; he has crossed over from death to life."

We live in a peculiar time. I feel that we are experiencing what is written in the book of Romans: "Therefore, God also gave them up to uncleanness, in the lusts of their hearts, to dishonor their bodies among themselves, who exchanged the truth of God for the lie, and worshiped and served the creature rather than the Creator, who is blessed forever. Amen." (1:24-25)

Has our society digressed to the culture of 58 A.D? Are we so deluded that we would not heed the warnings of God's own Word? This phenomenon is not peculiar to the USA; it appears to be popular cancerous rebellion against God.

AN ERA OF PROGRESSION OR REGRESSION?

Are we so progressive that we accept the *diversity, equity, and inclusion (DEI)* movement being figuratively shoved down our throats?

Diversity refers to the representation or composition of various social identity groups in a work group, organization, or community.

Equity involves providing resources according to the need to help diverse populations achieve their highest state of health and other functioning.

Inclusion strives for an environment that offers affirmation, celebration, and appreciation of different approaches, styles, perspectives, and experiences.

Is there a problem with the way our government is implementing these seemingly harmless movements? The answer is undeniably YES! My main issue with this "Program" is that those who are implementing it do not hold to the God-fearing values of our Founding Fathers. I agree all people should be equally represented. What possibly began as a worthy and equitable idea has been bushwacked by politics. They have created a new category of individuals who need to be represented; the LGBTQ+ groups. They have been massively embraced by elitest politicians whose only goal is to increase their pool of voters. In their endeavors to include all Americans, they have trampled the rights of many young and promising female athletes. They have trampled the privacy of locker rooms, restrooms, and classrooms. They have trampled the rights of business owners; the list goes on and on. My point is it is an abomination! It goes against the principles on which this great nation was founded. The Word of God has been ignored for too long. There is no direction for this once great nation to go but downward in free-fall. We desperately need to turn things around before it is too late!

WHAT DOES THE BIBLE SAY?

"You shall not lie with a male as with a woman; it is an abomination." (Leviticus 18:22)

"A woman shall not wear a man's garment, nor shall a man put on a woman's cloak, for whoever does these things is an abomination to the Lord your God." (Deuteronomy 22:5)

"If a man lies with a male as he lies with a woman, both of them have committed an abomination. They shall surely be put to death. Their blood shall be upon them." (Leviticus 20:13)

Genesis tells us God made us male and female to be His image-bearers. That means His decision to give us gendered bodies wasn't arbitrary. Nor was it just for practical reasons like making babies. It was necessary so that we could have the capacity to bear his image. That's why Christians can't join our culture in re-defining gender as a social construct. God has given our gendered-existence *eternal* significance.

"So God created humankind in his own image, in the image of God he created them; male and female he created them." (Genesis 1:27)

There is absolutely no doubt that the Christian message stands or falls upon the authenticity or spuriousness of the Bible. Believing it to be God's Word, millions across history have staked their very lives upon it, destiny-defining trust has been placed on it, graveside hope has been based upon it, extraordinary good has been spread because of it, the charters of nations have been built upon it, others with equal intensity have sought to expel it, yet wrongheaded zeal has caused untold evil in its name. There is no book in history that has been so studied, so used and so abused as the Holy Bible. How life inspiring it would be for so many more if only they could be indubitably certain of its truth. Can we muster the courage to face up to its claims of divine authorship?

WHAT IS THE BIBLE?

"All Scripture is God-breathed and is useful for teaching, rebuking, correcting, and training in righteousness." 2 Timothy 3:16

The Old Testament was written over 3000 years ago. The New Testament was written about 2000 years ago. Since that time, the original writings (manuscripts) have been copied over and over so they could be preserved and distributed to various locations. Thousands of manuscripts have been copied through the years. Many of them can still be found in international universities and museums.

As people around the world became Christians, they wanted to have the Bible translated into their own language. For centuries, the most used translation was Latin. Then in the 1300's, John Wycliff did the first entire Bible translation into English. However, he only translated from Latin to English. Then, in the 1600's, the King James Version (so named because he authorized it) was translated into English from the original languages, in which it was written, by a number of scholars working together.

Since then, there have been many other translations into English. Some of the progress was based on new manuscript discoveries during the last 400 years. However, most translation is a difficult process, so there are always different opinions regarding wording.

Some of the more recent English translations are the

Revised Standard Version (1952), The Living Bible (1962, which is actually a paraphrase rather than a translation), the New American Standard version (1971) and the New International Version (1978), the New King James Version (1982). Translation teams have worked hard to produce accurate and readable versions for English readers. This process still continues all over the world, by groups like Wycliff Bible Translators. The most recent revision of the NASB was published (2020)

The overall goal is to have an accurate and understandable translation from the original languages. This is not an easy task. So, find a reliable translation you can understand and dig in!

CHAPTER 7

Good Intentions vs. God's Intentions

You might be asking yourselves, "Why does our country and its values continue on a downward spiral?" In your heart of hearts, you know your only hope the only help is in God.

Hope doesn't come from predictions about the future, the promises of politicians, or the next new policy. Hope is found in the One Person who was born in a manger, died on a cross, rose from the tomb, and is coming again - Amen! Our only hope is found in our relationship with Jesus the Christ, God's only Son. Jesus came to the earth to suffer and die to save the world. God does not want one person to suffer eternity in hell's fire. Each of us, indeed, is an eternal being. Where do you wish to spend eternity?

The choice is ours; we all need to surrender our trust and our lives to Jesus. That is the bottom line! When you turn to Jesus and repent for a sinful or unbelieving life and subsequently turn your life over to Jesus, a transformation will take place in your life. You will still be the unique person God created you to be. The weight of a sinful nature will be lifted from your shoulders. You will slowly begin to see life's situations from a new perspective.

GIVING MEANING TO LIFE

The question that the writer of the Book of Ecclesiastes seeks to answer is, "Is there any meaning to the time that I spend in this world?"

We etch on tombstones a person's name, the date they were born, the date they died, and perhaps an epitaph. Between these two poles of time, we live our lives. The basic question is, "Does my life have meaning, and the bigger question is, what is *God's* purpose for *my* life?"

Since the dawn of time, philosophers and everyday people alike have pondered the idea of a "life purpose." In simplest terms, a life purpose is your reason (or reasons) for getting out of bed in the morning.

True purpose can guide your decisions. Purpose can offer a sense of direction and create meaning. For some people, purpose is connected to a vocation that is meaningful and satisfying work.

Now, after you have pondered or struggled with what is meaningful and satisfying, you need to tackle the biggest and greatest question of all; What is *God's* purpose for my life?

Are you confident that you know and are fulfilling God's purpose for your life? Have you ever considered what God has for you? I trust you are, but not everyone is reflecting on God's intentions. In our chaotic and unsettling world, it is sometimes hard to understand how God's purposes are being worked out in our lives. Whatever your case, in the midst of the confusion, fears, anxieties, and distractions of this present world, all of us can benefit from a firmer confidence that God is indeed working out His plans in our lives.

How can we gain this confidence? To be sure, we can't work it out on our own through human optimism and positive thinking. Rather, it is produced by the Holy Spirit, who works primarily (though not exclusively) through Holy Scripture, which He uses to enlighten our minds and kindle faith in our hearts. "So, then faith comes by hearing, and hearing by the Word of God." (Rom. 10:17)

A common refrain echoed in Ecclesiastes is that there is futility, vanity, and *"nothing new under the sun."* When we cease to look "under the sun" and seek our destiny "under heaven," we find our purpose.

The origins of mankind did not come about in some sort of *primordial soup* but in the very hands of God, who shaped us and breathed life into us. Our destiny is not to return to dust, but to give honor and praise to God forever. Under heaven we find purpose. If we have God as our origin and as our destiny, between those poles of our lifetime there is purpose and meaning.

Are you living your life "under the sun" or are you living your life "under heaven?" Have you found your true purpose and meaning to life?

FAITH, WHAT IS IT AND WHERE CAN I FIND IT?

Faith – what is faith? Faith is defined as belief with strong conviction; firm belief in something for which there may be no tangible proof; complete trust, confidence, reliance, or devotion. Faith is the opposite of doubt. Faith has two parts to it, and both are equally important.

The first part is belief: belief that God exists, that He loves us, and that He sent His Son into the world to save us. Faith isn't a vague hope that God might exist; it is a definite belief that what the Bible says about Him is true. The Bible says: "Without faith it is impossible to please God, because anyone who comes to him must believe that he exists and that he rewards those who earnestly seek him." (Hebrews 11:6)

The second part of faith is commitment: a definite decision not only to believe in our minds that Christ can save us, but to put our lives into His hands and trust Him alone for our salvation. True faith not only believes Christ can save us, but actually trusts Him to do it. The Bible says: "For it is by grace you have been saved, through faith." (Ephesians 2:8)

What is faith? Hebrews 11:1 says, "Now faith is the substance of things hoped for, the evidence of things not seen."

Faith is a concrete belief, built upon the assurance that God is faithful to His Word.

The following are a couple of examples of what faith is:

Someone once said: "When fear knocks at the door of the heart, send faith to open it, and you will find that there is no one there." Faith is what drives fear away! Because of fear in their lives - they come knocking at our door and ask, "Where can I find faith?"

Three boys once gave their definition of faith:

One said: Faith is taking hold of God.

The second said: Faith is holding on to God.

The third said: Faith is not letting go.

Three different answers, and yet each answer was accurate!

I found another illustration that can help us understand what faith is. During World War II, some escaped American prisoners of war hid in darkness for some time in a cellar in Cologne, Germany. They wrote on the wall this inscription:

> I believe in the sun, even when it is not shining.
> I believe in love, even when feeling it not.
> I believe in God, even when He is silent.

God requires that we have faith. One reason He does so is because those who believe receive from God, and those who do not, many times do without. The fact is, some needs will never be met, some storms will never cease, and some giants will never be killed until we believe.

In the physical sense of sight, your vision is checked by the eye doctor. If you have twenty-twenty vision, you see clearly. In the spiritual sense of sight, the eye of love prevails.

Without your eyes you cannot see light; without ears you cannot hear sounds; you cannot smell aromas without the nose that God gave you; you cannot taste without the taste buds God gave you; and without smell, you cannot taste. God gives you faith so you can believe things not seen.

Jesus is the source of Living Water, The Light of the World, The Bread of Life, The Breath of Life.

What Can We Do as Christians?

Post Christianity is the situation when Christianity is no longer the dominant civil religion of a society that has gradually assumed values, cultures, and worldviews that are not necessarily Christian.

I'll admit, my jaw dropped slightly when I read this on a church website: Christianity is our way to God, but it's not the only way to God. God draws people in many ways, and He welcomes them all."

In a nutshell, this means that all religions, lifestyles, and beliefs should be accepted and approved as true and moral. The formal term for this is "All-roads-lead-to-God." This approach is religious pluralism, which is part of what many refer to as "Post Christianity," of late renamed Progressive Christianity.

According to the Presbyterian Panel Survey of 2012-2014, 45 percent of Presbyterian Church USA (PCUSA) Pastors strongly disagree or disagree that "only followers of Jesus Christ can be saved." How much more of a downward shift exists today?

The idea of a church welcoming everyone sounds good on the surface, because, first of all, we are all imperfect. Imperfect people are invited to attend as they are, but if we dig a little deeper, we discover that "all are welcome here" doesn't simply mean welcoming sinners into the church. It also means approving of their sin. It isn't just about acknowledging the differing viewpoints of others; it's about upholding *all viewpoints* as truth.

"After all," the argument goes, "every one of us is broken and messed up. Why should one messed-up person be able to tell another messed-up person that he or she is wrong?" For those who hold this view, any kind of exclusion feels harsh and cruel.

We are all broken people, yet God loves all of humanity and wants each of us to turn to Him in our brokenness and find His healing. We don't have to be perfect when we come to Jesus. God does not accept sinful behavior, but He is ready to forgive when we ask, repent, and turn away from our sin.

God allows all to come to His table through faith in Jesus, no matter their race, background, sex, or socioeconomic status. All are welcome at the table, but there's only one way to get there—and that way is Jesus. Jesus Himself said in the book of John 14:6 "I am the way and the truth and the life. No one comes to the Father except through me."

Jesus wasn't shy about exposing sin or speaking words that can seem a little harsh to us. He loved people enough to draw near to them, but His love went even deeper than that: He loved them enough to point out the sins that were destroying them and show them the truth that could transform their lives. His love didn't validate their lifestyles; it completely overhauled them with a Holy Spirit healing.

While the Gospel invites everyone to "come as you are," it doesn't settle for anyone staying that way. Today we often hear a false message of love that tells us, "You're OK the way you are." But the Gospel of love tells us the truth: "You're not OK as you are, but Jesus can heal and transform you."

As Christians we must both encourage believers to live in moral purity and express in word and deed Christ's love for the lost. Aware of the claims of God on every aspect of our lives, we must emphasize that we are called to holiness. To unbelievers we must reach out with compassion and humility. We must hold no malice toward those struggling with addictions of any kind, adulterers, fornicators, or fear of homosexuals and those struggling with sexual identity—such attitudes are not of Christ. At the same time, we must not condone sexual behavior, homosexual or heterosexual, that God has defined as sinful. We need to check ourselves; it is so easy to look down on those struggling with sin. Remember, we are all sinners. Jesus came to save the world, that not one should perish. Believers are covered by the blood of Christ.

Way back, in the past, we were basically intolerant of certain behaviors and lifestyles, they were deemed socially and/or morally unacceptable. As time went by, we were encouraged to tolerate those behaviors, however, gradually, and progressively we were encouraged to accept those behaviors and lifestyles. Before you know it, you will be labeled "closeminded" if you do not accept and embrace those behaviors and lifestyles. This is a classic path of digression. It is happening before our very eyes! Are we aware of what has happened and is happening? Over time, if you are not careful, you can passively become a part of the problem. We need to keep our minds and hearts alert to the chip, chip, chipping away at our thoughts and our values. Make no mistake, Satan is at work. Satan is no more powerful today than he was when he fell from heaven. Satan has no more control over our minds than what we are willing to allow, voluntarily or subconsciously.

We have our government and our educational systems giving preferential treatment to those behaviors and lifestyles we once only tolerated. We find ourselves being steamrolled by "society." Yes, we are a part of society and yes, we can blame it on society because we are in the least unaccepting, even against changes we see to society at large and all of this is silently whittling away at our democracy and our freedoms of expression. It all seems to be closing in around us and weighing us down, incrementally smothering the principles on which this nation was founded.

Living as a Christ follower in a post-Christian culture can be challenging. History tells us that when a nation abandons its moral and religious heritage it quickly moves from a post-Christian culture to an anti-Christian culture. That, my friends, is a description of the world we live in today. Furthermore, spiritual warfare is real and our enemy the devil would like nothing more than to see all Christian influences crushed in every part of the world. Scripture tells us this will happen (read the book of Revelation). In the last days the unbelieving world will literally fight against God and attempt to kill all who follow Him.

There are many places in the world where Christians must meet secretly, where people who come to salvation in Christ risk losing their family connections, their livelihoods, and even their lives. Thankfully, there are still places where we can openly worship God, but our society is becoming more and more intolerant of Christian beliefs.

How can we remain loyal to the truth in this post-Christian culture? What wisdom does Scripture offer? What should we expect and how can we prepare for what surely will come?

God's own Word tells us: "Be strong and courageous. Do not be afraid or terrified because of them, for the

Lord your God goes with you; he will never leave you nor forsake you." (Deuteronomy 31:6) God is still moving, God is still rescuing people, God will not leave you or forsake you.

"Let your conduct be without covetousness; be content with such things as you have. For He Himself has said, "I will never leave you nor forsake you." (Hebrews 13:5)

The Apostle Peter wrote his first epistle in just such an environment. In those days, the Roman empire was ruled by the insane Emperor, Nero. The outbreak of persecution of Christians began because of the great fire of AD 64 in Rome. Nero laid blame for the fire on Christians whom he already perceived as enemies of Rome because they would not worship him, as was demanded of all citizens of Rome. Christians would worship none but Christ.

The Apostles Peter and Paul were both martyred during Nero's unrestrained persecution, but not before Peter wrote his encouraging letter to the Christ-followers scattered across the known world. Throughout the centuries Christians under attack have benefited from the apostle's wise counsel and gentle encouraging words of comfort from the epistles written by Peter.

In his first epistle, Peter focuses on the importance of believers bearing up under unjust suffering yet continuing to live well. "But how is it to your credit if you receive a beating for doing wrong and endure it? But if you suffer for doing good and you endure it, this is commendable before God." (1 Peter 2:20)

Because of this, Peter might be called the Job of the New Testament, providing encouragement for true believers to continue living in the way that Jesus has laid out for all His followers. The endurance Peter called these believers to is like Job's, a man who suffered greatly despite his righteousness. Peter advocated that this was the kind of true perseverance that God expects from His people.

The Apostle Paul, also martyred during Nero's reign, never gave up or gave into the many trials he suffered during his ministry to the world of non-believers. Many were brought to Christ by the persevering witness of Paul. His encouragement to Christians suffering persecution during his time on earth and his words continue to be an encouragement to us in our post-modern culture and to fellow believers suffering in our world today. He wrote "For our citizenship is in heaven, from which we also eagerly wait for the Savior, the Lord Jesus Christ," (Philippians 3:20); and "Now then, we are ambassadors for Christ, as though God were pleading through us: we implore you on Christ's behalf, be reconciled to God." (2 Corinthians 5:20)

God has ordained the social institutions of family, church, and government for the benefit of mankind and as a reflection of His divine nature. Therefore, Christians are called to support these institutions, according to God's design and purpose, and to protect them against destructive social influences. Such involvement is in obedience to Christ's Lordship over all creation and is required by His command to care for the well-being of all people.

Genesis 2:24 says, "For this reason a man will leave his father and mother and be united to his wife, and they will become one flesh." God created the holy union of marriage. A man and a woman are joined together for the reason of procreation. Without God's plan, we, none of us would exist.

During these tumultuous times we must, as ambassadors for Christ, hold fast to the promises of God. We must draw nearer to Him. However, it is not enough to just draw near to Him. We must also hold fast to the confession of our hope. "Let us hold unswervingly to the hope we profess, for he who promised is faithful." (Hebrews 10:23)

However, it is not enough to draw near to Him. We must not worship God silently and in secret but must also display our allegiance to Him publicly. Here we see the close connection between true faith and outward practice that is highlighted on every page of the Bible. It is not enough to be silent and think that we have true faith if no one ever knows about it. Rather, true faith is only true faith if we believe in our hearts and confess with our lips. "That if you confess with your mouth the Lord Jesus and believe in your heart that God has raised Him from the dead, you will be saved." (Rom. 10:9) God requires also profession or confession; it is not true faith if we do not confirm our faith to others.

CHAPTER 8

Closing

THE WORLD WE USED TO KNOW

There is a song by Glen Campbell called "The World I Used to Know." A snippet of the lyrics says, "Someday the world I used to know, Will come along and bid me go."

Have we come so far that there is no turning back?

Think back to your earliest memory: you're three years old without a care in the world, just petting your dog or exploring the "enormous" world that is your home. Or maybe you're five and just beginning kindergarten where the only thing you should be concerned with is what crayon you're going to use to finish the work of art in your coloring book. Then you're six and heading off to first grade—homework and tests are your concerns— maybe Scouts or Karate. Progress to age nine, when girls or boys have "cooties" and late-night ghost stories are your worst fears.

It was much simpler times back then, nothing to worry about. The news? What of it? You were more concerned with what was happening in SpongeBob's life in Bikini Bottom. There was nothing to fear. Innocence—and ignorance—truly were bliss.

The world you used to know was a cheerful one. Everyone smiled at you and most always had something nice to say. Your mother or father tucked you in at night or read you a bedtime story. You didn't really observe the negative aspects; you were simply a happy-go-lucky kid, or maybe you just weren't exposed to it - who knows. Only your immediate surroundings were of interest to you, nothing farther than your backyard. Iran? That was nothing more than a sentence or the beginning of one, "I ran during recess yesterday."

But, alas, with growing up you begin to realize more and more about your surroundings as well as what actually goes on in the world around you - whether you want to know about it or not. The wool is slowly pulled back from shading your eyes. You may not watch or read the news at all, but you'll have a general knowledge about current things such as who's winning in the upcoming election, the various wars in the Middle East, who won an Oscar or Grammy and random "doom and gloom" tidbits from around the globe.

You notice more of the negative and blot out the positive. When you were young, everyone was always your biggest fan, always saying "you can!" regarding your dreams, but nowadays being a dreamer is looked down upon. More people are eager to tell you "No, you can't" and provide reasons to support their views as to why you can't and won't, because dreams are just that: dreams. The realists tend to outweigh the dreamers. What happened to all the support? The positivity that overflowed around you as a child? As the years progress, pessimism sets in. But why? Simply because people feed on cynicism. Just look at any newscast or newspaper headline. Typically, it's not something cheerful and "happy." No, it tends to revolve around negativity: violence, human trafficking, wars, terrorism, slander, scandals, theft, hatred. Those types of stories are far more interesting, however, as more and more negativity is put into the spotlight, it may trigger another person to believe that if he does something equally as terrible, if not worse, then he, too can get that headline, thus creating a sequence of more terrible deeds, a chain reaction, as it were.

This world is changing day by day, hour by hour, second by second. It's a dark place out there, nowadays. There is so much more to worry about now that we're older and understand the world better. But who's to say the world must stay this way? Who's to say we need to let the negativity of the media dictate our outlooks on the world or even life as whole? The only way to counteract the negative is with a positive. Yes, the world we live in is pretty blah, but that can change. And it all starts with one person.

It's time to get back to "the world we used to know."

When it feels as though we are hedged in on every side by a culture that is attacking our Christian beliefs, we must seek wisdom in Scripture. It's what we as Christians do.

And as you know, the apostle Paul had all kinds of wisdom. As a missionary, he traveled to countries that had beliefs entirely counter to his and he turned them toward God. From him, you can learn how to do the same in our society today. Read the story of Paul on

Mars Hill, speaking to the Greeks about their "unknown god" and using their foundational philosophies to bring them to truth and Jesus in Acts 17:16-34. Mars Hill is the location of one of Paul's most important gospel presentations during his visit to Athens in his second missionary journey. There, he addressed their false beliefs concerning the altar of an "Unknown God." It was this altar and their religious idolatry that Paul used as a starting point to present the gospel message to them. Paul proclaimed the one true God and taught the people how they may be reconciled.

Eradication of Christian principles and Christian ethics is exactly what has brought our country to its knees. However, either our political elitists with loud voices are hiding the truth or they are completely blind to the truth. Have their minds been "dulled"? Are they nothing more than pawns in play by the hand of Satan himself? Many of the so-called, prominent public figures have ascribed to discounting of the voice of Christianity, and some have even gone so far as to show preference to the laws and traditions of other religions, in direct conflict with the will and Word of God.

Our young people and many of the older, as well, have adopted the ideology of those within this group, with a public platform, the world view, as the truth. Today, truth has evolved from the absolute to a state of relativity. This way of thinking has virtually poisoned the minds of many, perhaps even the majority, of the citizens of this once fine, prosperous, and virtuous country. Conservative college students have a target on their backs. Fellow students shout them down or freeze them out, as if their points of view are irrelevant.

This, my friends, is a slippery slope. Have we still not learned from history? Are we destined to suffer the consequences that led to the downfall of virtually all kingdoms and all empires of the world, since the beginning of time? Our children are being taught by history revisionists who have been taught by college professors whose goal seems to be bent on destroying our once great and God-fearing country.

We are a stiff-necked civilization, not unlike the Egyptian Empire whose Pharaoh chose to ignore the will of God, even though ten plagues were visited upon the citizens of Egypt. The stubbornness of Pharaoh led to the total annihilation of the Egyptian Army and the successful exodus of the Israelites from Egypt. The crowns of every kingdom of the past lay in the dust of the earth and all the empires of old have stumbled and crumbled. Can we now learn from times gone by, from the mistakes made in the name of progress?

How quickly we forget that was not the end of the story for the Israelites. They too, chose to ignore the will of God and the result was forty-years of wandering through the wilderness until an entire generation had passed before God delivered them to the Promised Land.

Did they learn their lesson from all of this? We, as parents, must pass on to our children the truth and never let them forget it. Do not let history revisionists, socialists, and atheists feed their lies to your children. Our children and generations to come must know the truth.

The ideas that shaped our culture were great and worthy. Our Forefathers had a goal, to reconcile liberty with law. But in the last century our culture has undergone incredible changes and challenged the ideas that once shaped and guided us. The result has been the collapse of law, the eradication of the Holy Spirit, and the unleashing of evil.

The response of the Christian calling for a return to morality is nothing more than a scream into the dark. Our screams seem to not be heard. It is as if we are screaming into the dark because morality has no self-sustaining light.

Yet, our great country was founded by the Divine Providence of God. Men and women of faith, fleeing from tyranny, risking it all, were guided here by the hand of our Creator.

There are many people who cling to what they have in this world, for they are oblivious to God's promises. Since they do not consider the reality of God, they are open to believe the lies and half-truths that swirl around them. The world is overflowing with lies of one sort or another. The devil does not care what lies we believe as long as we do not believe the truth.

Perhaps they have heard the truth of God and who He is, and they think the gospel is overblown hype. Only with truth and the authority of the Word of God can morality be anchored, evil understood, and the soul restored.

We, as a country, need to take stock in the Will of God and the Word of God, or we, as those who have gone before us, will most definitely suffer the consequences. His promise is true. He will never leave us or forsake us.

"If my people, who are called by my name, will humble themselves and pray and seek my face and turn from their wicked ways, then I will hear from heaven, and I will forgive their sin and will heal their land." (2 Chronicles 7:14)

It is as simple as told in the verse above. God's plan for mankind is a simple one. Apparently, there are too many simple-minded influencers among the flock.

There is always hope. Think about it, what gives you hope?

What gives me hope are Paul's wonderful words in Philippians 1:20 "As it is my eager expectation and hope that I will not be at all ashamed, but that with full courage now as always, Christ will be honored in my body, whether by life or by death."

Paul also says in Romans 14:8 says, "For if we live, we live to the Lord, and if we die, we die to the Lord. So then, whether we live or whether we die, we are the Lord's.

The city of Jerusalem was surrounded by a wall, as were many cities. The wall would protect the cities from danger. Atop those walls were guards watching out for any threat that might come from marauders, thieves, and hostile forces.

"On your walls, O Jerusalem, I have set watchmen; all the day and all the night they shall never be silent. You who put the Lord in remembrance, take no rest." (Isaiah 62:6)

Those of us who know the Truth, we are the Watchman on the wall. We must sound the warning, that none should perish.

"I appeal to you, brothers, to watch out for those who cause divisions and create obstacles contrary to the doctrine that you have been taught; avoid them." (Romans 16:17)

The bottom line is: Without Jesus in your life and your heart, you will never be what God created you to be.

Printed in the USA
CPSIA information can be obtained
at www.ICGtesting.com
JSHW080952071023
49713JS00001B/91